who do you think you are?

by tucker shaw

12 methods for analyzing the true you

alloyBooks

To the Rays, for reminding me how sad life would be if we were all the same.

Muchas gracias to Susan Kaplow for believing in me.

Thanks to Angie, Fiona, Lauren, Deb, and the Queen for helping me figure out what this book should be.

Big props to Jodi Anderson for being so dang smart.

Love to Lauren Monchik for bringing this sucker to life, not to mention the rest of the staff at 17th Street Productions.

Mad gratitude to Chuck Gonzalez for his killer illustrations.

Shout out to Joy Peskin and the rest of the Penguin crew. (Thanks, y'all!)

Hats off to Matt Diamond, Sam Gradess, and Jim Johnson for making this whole thing possible.

And most of all, thanks to everyone I've ever met, anytime, anywhere.

ALLOY BOOKS
Published by the Penguin Group
Penguin Putnam Books for Young Readers,
345 Hudson Street, New York, New York 10014, U.S.A.

Published by Puffin Books,
a division of Penguin Putnam Books for Young Readers, 2001

10 9 8 7 6 5 4 3 2

Illustrations by Chuck Gonzalez/Arts Council
Calligraphy on pages 30-45 by Amy Mu
Cover and interior design by Lauren Monchik

 Produced by 17th Street Productions,
an Alloy Online, Inc. company
33 West 17th Street
New York, NY 10011

ISBN 0-14-131091-x
Printed in the United States of America

intro

OKAY, BEFORE YOU START THINKING THAT THIS
book is going to give you The Big Secret to who you are and
what kind of life you're going to have, forget it. This book won't
do that. No book will do that. Ever. You're just too unique. Trust
me, I know better than to try and pin you down.

What I *am* going to do, though, is give you some stuff to think
about. Stuff that'll help you make some sense of yourself and the
people around you. There are twelve systems in this book that'll
help you do it, like *numerology*, which uses your birth date to give
a reading on what you're good at and what your challenges are.
Like the *seven types of intelligence*, which takes a look at how your
brain works and helps to explain why you might love third-period
English but hate sixth-period algebra. Or like the *enneagram*,
which charts your personal characteristics and gauges how you
interact with others. And more.

All of these systems will give you clues to who you are, who
you're compatible with, and why you look at life the way you do.
They'll also remind you about parts of yourself that you *don't* like.
But most important, they'll be fun. Actually, a lot of fun.

4

There will be times in this book where I'm all, "You're *this!*" and you'll be all, "*Yeah!* I'm totally *this!*" But there will also be times when you'll be all, "I'm not like that!" Just remember: Even when a certain analysis isn't quite on target, it'll still give you something to chew on. It's kind of a jumping-off point for finding out more about yourself.

And that's what this whole book is for: to get you thinking about who you are—*and* who you aren't.

Oh, and there's more. You can use this stuff to decode your friends, family, and other people in your life, too. Like my dad is a Rooster in Chinese astrology (page 43) and, well, it explains a lot. (Hi, Dad.) Oh, and this English teacher I had in high school—I utterly couldn't stand him . . . until I realized he was a Capricorn (page 142) and I figured out how to deal with him. So if you need help understanding someone in your life (your dad or a teacher or anyone else), you've come to the right place.

Anyway, you get the idea. Have fun with this book, and pay attention. There's good stuff in here.

later,
tucker

what's your number?

HUMAN BEINGS HAVE BEEN USING NUMBERS TO understand personalities (and tell the future) for as long as they've kept records. Ancient Mesopotamian, Egyptian, Hindu, Chinese, and Mayan civilizations (you know, the ones that come at the *beginning* of your ancient history textbook) paid very close attention to the relationship between numbers and personality. Turns out that numbers have always been used for more than trig exams and phone digits—if you manipulate them right, they can give you something to think about on the personality tip.

Give it a shot. Go ahead and calculate your number using this system (it's easy . . . no calculator necessary), then read up.

All it takes is breaking down all the numbers in your birth date and adding them together; keep doing it until you're down to one digit. Let's use, uh, Prince William's birthday as an example. . . .

Birthday:	*June 21, 1982*
Converted to digits:	*6/21/1982*
Add it all together:	*6+2+1+1+9+8+2=29*
Break it down and	
add again:	*2+9=11*
And again:	*1+1=2*
Prince William's number:	*2 (see page 10)*

Got it? Let's do another. How about, oh, what the hell, Britney Spears?

Birthday:	*December 2, 1981*
Converted to digits:	*12/2/1981*
Add it all together:	*1+2+2+1+9+8+1=24*
Break it down and	
add again:	*2+4=6*
Britney Spears's	
number:	*6 (see page 14)*

Easy, right?
Okay, your turn.

So You're a 1

Key word: *Aware*
You rule because: You're self-assured, independent, and unique.
But sometimes: You're arrogant.

about you:

Cliché alert: Just like the number 1, you're one of a kind. You're never afraid to say what you feel or to stand up for yourself. Even if your point of view isn't popular, you're comfortable standing alone if necessary. You're unique, and even though you sometimes surprise even yourself with just *how* unique you can be, your confidence in your personality—and the creativity that goes along with it—will only grow as you go through life.

your challenge: to be less of a control freak

Being the leader of your posse comes naturally to you, but so does being harsh on others. Sure, you're full of new and interesting ideas (and some really rad looks), and you get such good reactions from people that you kind of expect everyone else to follow you wherever you feel like taking them. But when they disagree or when they want to take their own path, you get annoyed. What's that about? Remember, just because you speak for yourself so well, that doesn't necessarily mean you can speak for everyone else.

So You're a 2

Key word: *Understanding*
You rule because: You're friendly, social, and communicative.
But sometimes: You're insecure.

about you:

Hey, flirter. Quit batting those eyelashes and listen up. You're the ulti-mate social butterfly, bouncing from chic clique to freak clique and back again with no kind of trouble. You're in touch with all sorts of people—not just because you hang out with them, but because you *listen* to what they have to say. You're friendly, and people always remember meeting you—you're the kind of person who makes everyone feel important. Oh, and you're a heartbreaker. But hey, there just aren't enough days in the year to go out with everyone who wants a date.

your challenge: to learn to say no

There's someone you've been neglecting lately, number 2. Who? *You.* Yes, you've spent so much time helping other peo-ple, being there when they need you, and figuring out new ways to impress them that you've totally blown off yourself and ignored the stuff you wanted to do, the goals you wanted to accomplish. You gotta learn to say no sometimes when people ask you to do stuff or at least, "Maybe later."

So You're a 3

Key word: *Self-expressive*
You rule because: You're enthusiastic, optimistic, and creative.
But sometimes: You're scatterbrained.

about you:

Hello, imagination. You're the most artistically focused number, number 3—if you're not a painter, you're probably taking snapshots, humming new melodies, wearing unique outfits, doodling, hanging out at one of those paint-your-own-pottery places; you know . . . creative stuff like that. Your emotions inspire you rather than frighten or bother you—you *feel* things majorly, but you don't let them bring you down. Because of this you've got a lot to say and a lot of cool ideas for how to say it.

your challenge: to get organized

You've got a lot going on in your head—and if you had your way, you'd spend all day thinking it all over. Sorry, you can't. See, there's a world going on and a life to lead, and if you want to make it happen, you need to get organized. You can't set a free-throw record unless you show up on game day outfitted and practiced. Get on the ball, number 3 . . . you've got the talent.

So You're a 4

Key word: *Physical*
You rule because: You're practical, patient, and dependable.
But sometimes: You're stubborn.

about you:

You wake up every morning, number 4, and you know exactly what the day will bring. And even if life hits you with something unexpected, you'll figure out why it happened and how to deal. See, you're practical, which means that whatever you do with your time better have a purpose, or you probably won't bother. You're incredibly helpful to other people, and even though you don't always show it, you love making a difference in others' lives. You're loyal, dependable, and prepared for any- and everything. Oh, and you're handy with a toolbox. You can fix stuff. That rules.

your challenge: to be more open-minded

You may think that just because they admire your ability to deal with anything and just because they truly *need* you, other people will try and, well, *be* more like you. But they don't, and when they don't, you get annoyed. Well, check it out, number 4: They aren't you, and they never will be. And think about it—as much as they need you . . . don't you need them, too? Remember: Everyone's got just as much value as you do.

So You're a 5

Key word: *Instinctive*
You rule because: You're ingenious, independent, and sensible.
But sometimes: You're inconsistent.

about you:

You never have a hard time making a decision, do you? Your instincts always seem to get you where you need to go—and you go a lot of places! Freedom and independence are important to you, and life's challenges (big and little) are what keep you getting up in the morning. You're a born entrepreneur—inventive enough to come up with big idea after big idea and enthusiastic enough to get people psyched about every single one. And thanks to your straight-up common sense, you can be sure your big ideas won't be impossible.

your challenge: to be consistent

Face facts, number 5: You can be a real flake sometimes. Okay, maybe that's harsh, but seriously—people never know from one day to the next what new idea or project you're gonna be all revved up about. Try some consistency. People look for it when they're looking for someone to trust. Now, you're definitely trustworthy, but people might not know it because you're also, well, all over the place. Prove yourself by being consistent about something. Anything.

tucker says

I'm a 5. Always have been. It's the only thing I've really been consistent about yet. That and having a big new idea every single day.

So You're a 6

Key word: *Involved*
You rule because: You're trustworthy, compassionate, and you love people.
But sometimes: You're critical.

about you:

You're a truly idealistic person, number 6—if the whole world were nothing but 6s it would be a peaceful, compassionate place indeed. *Visionary* and *humanitarian* are words that people use (or will use) to describe you, along with *supportive* and *inspiring*. You're the kind of person who's first in line to congratulate someone on their achievements, and you probably brought refreshments for everyone else in the line, too. Family is incredibly important to you, and you'll be an awesome parent one day.

your challenge: to mind your own business

You'd do anything to make things easier on everyone. Empathy is your middle name. Yep, you *care* about people—maybe too much. As in, you can be one nosy number when you really want to be. See, just because you want the best for someone doesn't mean you need to get all up in their business. It's not just sharing that makes people live together peacefully—it's giving people some space every now and then.

So You're a 7

Keyword: *Intuitive*
You rule because: You're brainy, intuitive, and honest.
But sometimes: You're self-absorbed.

about you:

Hey, brainiac! Yeah, you! Face it, you're book-smart, street-smart, all kindsa smart. See, you've got a talent for blending your strong intuition with your powerful intellect, which enables you to analyze and understand any situation—from final exams to the Final Four basketball pool. You like to investigate everything—and your natural curiosity means you've got more info stored up there in your head than most.

your challenge: to learn to communicate more clearly

Sure, your brain can take in any piece of information in the world and make sense of it, but can you understand what's going on inside you and communicate it to others? You're as honest as it gets, but sometimes you don't know exactly how to get your message across—or even what the message should be. And it makes you feel a little isolated. Get in touch with yourself, and you'll get in touch with others. Find a friend and spill your guts. Just make sure you pick a good listener.

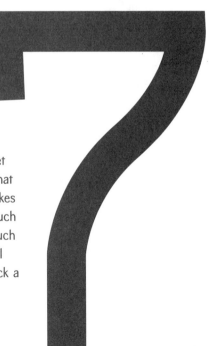

So You're an 8

Key word: *Motivated*

You rule because: You're strong, direct, and hardworking.

But sometimes: You're impatient.

about you:

You might as well start your presidential campaign now. No, not class president. I'm talking Oval Office, West Wing, White House. See, you're the ultimate leader: strong, fair, ambitious, and dedicated. Am I exaggerating? Okay, maybe. But not all that much. You've got a great sense of judgment. You know how to manage things, especially your own life. Don't believe it now? Wait and see . . . your organizational skills will only get better as your life goes on.

your challenge: to be considerate of others

News flash! Not everyone's as organized and complete as you are. And you know what? That's okay. See, the thing is, you care so much about what happens and how it happens that sometimes you forget that other people might want to do things differently. Open up your mind, number 8, and let people live their own lives the way *they* want to. Oh, and practice saying this: "I forgive you." You need to say it more.

So You're a 9

Key word: *Compassionate*
You rule because: You're kind, tolerant, and idealistic.
But sometimes: You're moody.

about you:

You're all about bringing people together—sticking with just one clique has never been your style. You're generous, open-minded, and supportive, and people are always asking for your awesome advice. Popular doesn't begin to describe what you are—you don't even play games like that; you just like everyone and they like you. You'll need to travel and meet a lot of people in your life to stay interested, and you will.

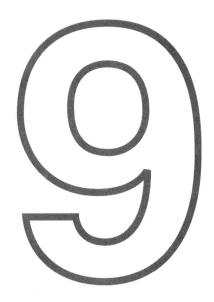

your challenge: to be realistic

You have such high hopes for yourself and everyone around you, and you see such good qualities in everyone you meet, that sometimes you're kind of unrealistic about the way the world really is. You'd rather not hear the bad news than have to figure out how to deal with it. But surprise—stuff happens. Remember that, and check yourself next time you believe everything's just perfect. Not to burst your bubble, but nothing ever is. Oh, and that's okay.

Check page 157 for where to find out more about numerology.

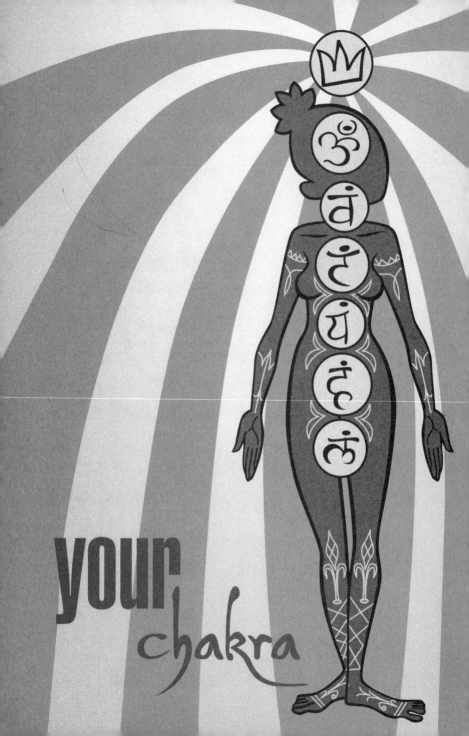

your chakra

what's your chakra vibe?

THE CHAKRAS ARE A SACRED ELEMENT OF HINDU
tradition, used by millions of people around the world. For thousands
of years people have been working with the chakras to help understand themselves and their relationships to the rest of the universe.

The chakras are, in one sense, seven stages that your soul or
spirit goes through during your lifetime (and beyond). Think of the
seven chakras as a ladder. As you go through life, as you mature and
learn more about yourself and your place in the universe, you move
up from one chakra to the next. (You can also move back down.)

On a physical level the chakras are seven points on your body,
each representing one of your spiritual stages. The first chakra is
down at the base of your spine, the second is down there in your
business, the third just above your stomach, and so on. Each of these
spots is considered an energy center— where you can focus energy
(usually during meditation) to get in touch with that particular chakra.

As you read the following descriptions, try to pinpoint which chakra
is strongest in your life or which chakra you're currently "in." If you see
a problem you're struggling with, it might be an obstacle that's keeping
you from "graduating" from that chakra.

the first chakra: Muladhara
the root chakra

key word: *Survival*
location: Base of spine
color: Red
your motivation here: Survival and food
first-chakra problems: Eating disorders and insomnia
characteristics: This is the chakra that's closest to the ground. It represents your most basic connection to the earth and to life. This chakra is all about doing what you need to do to stay alive and not much more. Eat, sleep, eat, sleep. People who live primarily through this chakra focus on themselves and only themselves. When you move beyond this chakra, you hit:

the second chakra: Svadhistara
the sex chakra

key word: *Intimacy*
location: Genitals
color: Orange
your motivation here: Sex
second-chakra problems: Sexual obsessions and body-image worries (but not eating disorders, which stay within the first chakra)
characteristics: The second chakra is all about being close to other people—relationships, intimacy, and warmth. Some people say this chakra is all about reproduction, but it's also about sharing experiences, space, and time with other human beings. People living in this chakra focus a lot on relationships and sex. Okay, I'll get real: They focus more on sex than on relationships. Get past this chakra for:

the third chakra: Manipura
the power chakra

key word: *Independence*
location: Solar plexus (just above the stomach)
color: Yellow
your motivation here: Knowledge and relationships
third-chakra problems: Insecurity and codependence
characteristics: Willpower, choice, and independence are at the core of this chakra. It's about understanding yourself as someone who can *do* stuff and make a difference—to yourself and to the world. This book is a kind of third-chakra experience since it's all about figuring out who you are, what you're about, and how you relate to everyone else. Logic, reason, and thinking all hang here. But there's even more to life, like:

the fourth chakra: Anahata
the heart chakra

key word: *Love*
location: Heart
color: Green
your motivation here: Compassion and unconditional love
fourth-chakra problems: Isolation and depression
characteristics: This is the chakra that takes you to that place where you actually "feel" someone else's pain—or happiness. Some people call it compassion, some call it empathy, but neither of those words really explains the burning sensation you feel in this chakra when you're truly moved by love. Very few people actually live in this chakra (think Mother Teresa), and even fewer make it to:

the fifth chakra: Vishuddha
the mind chakra

key word: *Awareness*
location: Throat
color: Sky blue
your motivation here: Connection and understanding
fifth-chakra problems: Faithlessness and disconnectedness
characteristics: This is the hardest chakra to explain, but it's about recognizing yourself as an integral part of the rest of the universe. Just like your family wouldn't be the same without you, the whole entire universe wouldn't be the same without you, either. See? Truly understanding this concept doesn't happen up in your brain; it happens with your whole body—it's like each cell in you says, "Ah, I get it," and means it. This is the chakra that people try to focus on to spark creativity and imagination. This is just about the limit for any spirit on this planet, except for a superselect few who find themselves on their way to:

the sixth chakra: Ajna
the third eye

key word: *Wisdom*
location: Between the brows
color: Indigo
your motivation here: Enlightenment
sixth-chakra problems: Self-identity (In this chakra that's a bad thing. By now you should be past it, considering yourself as part of the universe, not as an individual. Actually, if you're truly in this chakra, you probably shouldn't be considering yourself at all.)
characteristics: Think of the person you go to when you're down, the one who not only solves your problem but also knows what to say, just how to hug you, and exactly what kind of Ben & Jerry's you want after you cry. Now, multiply what this person does for you by a million billion. Spirits who get to this chakra are so aware and comfortable with their place in the universe that they no longer identify themselves with

their bodies—in other words, they're selfless and connected to everything and everybody. They see deeper and farther than the rest of us with their third eye, represented by the bindi. (The third eye, located between the other two, sees things that normal eyes can't, things like truth, enlightenment, and, yes, chakras.) And if they were to take it even further, like if they were the Buddha, they'd rise to:

the seventh chakra: Sahasrara
the crown chakra

key word: *Enlightenment*
location: Top of the head
color: Violet
your motivation here: None
seventh-chakra problems: None
characteristics: This chakra is the connection point to nirvana, or a state of perfection. It's about ultimate connection, understanding, and love for the universe. When a person has ascended this far, a spirit ceases to be physical and transforms itself into light and energy. In fact, it's almost silly to talk about this chakra with words because according to ancient Hindu texts, it's absolutely indescribable.

so, what chakra are you living in?
Okay, I take the question back. It's not especially useful to try and plug yourself into a particular chakra because you'd never want to identify yourself too strongly with one of them—you always want to be flexible enough to move to the next level. But thinking about the chakras and paying attention to what's going on in your life can help you figure out where you're headed.

tucker says
I'm probably sitting pretty in the third chakra. But sometimes, late at night, I pretend I'm in the seventh.

Check page 156 for where to find out more about chakras.

your BODYTYPE

what does your BODY TYPE say about you?

STOP! BEFORE YOU START THINKING THAT THIS section is about ideal bodies, or which kind of body is hottest, or whatever else you might have in mind when you hear the words *body type*, let me tell you: This section is about something completely different. It has nothing to do with your attractiveness or anything like that. Okay?

This section *is* about how your basic body shape can give you clues to your personality and how your mind and body relate. I'm not talking about fat and skinny, or hot and not hot, or sexy and unsexy, or anything like that. I'm talking about your skeleton, your posture, your limbs and joints—the way you're constructed. Most of us fall into one of three basic categories, all of which have plusses and minuses—mentally, emotionally, and physically.

Where'd I get this stuff? This system dates back to the 1940s. William Sheldon came up with the three types, but he was always saying that everyone has parts of all three in them. Most people have one type that's more dominant, but not always. In other words, it's a fuzzy system, meant to get you thinking, not define you.

Go close the door, take off all your clothes, and look in the mirror. (It's okay; no one's watching. I did it, too.) Stand back several feet and squint a little so you can focus on the general shape of your body instead of that zit on your forehead. Look hard, then take your eyes away and look again to make sure you get it right.

Then take a look at the three body types that follow. Which looks most like your body? (Remember, these won't look *exactly* like you.)

FAMOUS ENDOMORPHS
Missy Elliott
Nick Carter

FAMOUS MESOMORPHS
Britney Spears
Enrique Iglesias

FAMOUS ECTOMORPHS
Cameron Diaz
Ashton Kutcher

ENDOMORPH

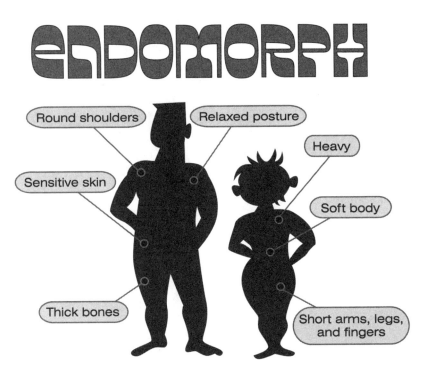

Round shoulders

Relaxed posture

Heavy

Sensitive skin

Soft body

Thick bones

Short arms, legs, and fingers

The upside: You endomorphs tend to be kind, funny, friendly, and relaxed. You really like people, and they like you, too. You're in a good mood most of the time, but even when you aren't, it won't be long until you are. You love meeting new people and having new experiences. You love finding new ways to have fun and enjoy life, and the best part? You love to share that life. If you're lucky enough to be an endo-morph, you're probably surrounded by friends 24/7—cooking, eating, drinking, chilling, and making plans.

The downside: There's a reason you surround yourself with friends—it's because you crave the attention. When you don't get the attention you need, you feel isolated and frustrated. Also, endomorphs should keep an eye on weight-related health issues . . . especially later in life.

MESOMORPH

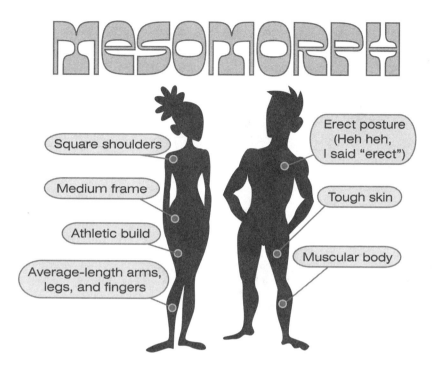

Square shoulders

Medium frame

Athletic build

Average-length arms, legs, and fingers

Erect posture (Heh heh, I said "erect")

Tough skin

Muscular body

The upside: You mesomorphs are generally active, adventurous, and brave. You love to use your body for sports, dancing, and spending time outdoors. While you're very open to different people and ideas, you don't often follow the pack—you like to make up your own mind about things. To most mesomorphs, the mind and the body aren't separate things—they're a single unit.

tucker says

Most people exhibit characteristics of all three body types, but usually one is the most obvious. Like me. I'm a mesomorph. But like ectomorphs, I love being alone, and like endomorphs, I like to cook. Wanna come over for dinner?

The downside: You might be kind of a space case sometimes and maybe self-centered. You love to compete—in sports, in school, in life—but sometimes you can go a little hard on your opponents. Oh, and some mesomorphs pay too much attention to the body and appearance—are you one of them?

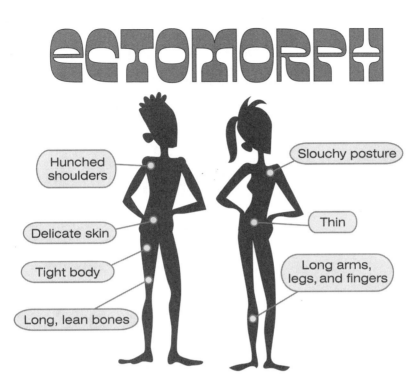

ECTOMORPH

- Hunched shoulders
- Slouchy posture
- Delicate skin
- Thin
- Tight body
- Long arms, legs, and fingers
- Long, lean bones

The upside: You ectomorphs are smart, creative, and very talented. You've got a good sense of direction. You know what's going on around you, who's nearby, and exactly how much gas is in the tank. You probably spend lots of time getting to know yourself and understanding what's going on inside you. You probably love this book. You probably like spending time alone, even though you love your friends, too. People come to you for advice a lot because you're a great listener.

The downside: If you're like most ectomorphs, you probably hold back your emotions a lot, keeping certain parts of yourself very private . . . which is fine, but sometimes others can't figure out what your deal is. You might be sensitive, and you probably have a hard time taking criticism. Oh, and do you tend to get a lot of colds?

Check page 156 for where to find out more about body types.

what's your
chinese animal?

OKAY, SO YOU'VE HEARD OF ARIES AND GEMINI (more on them later). But what do you know about the Rat and the Ox?

The Chinese astrological system is as old as Western astrology (or maybe even older—it's impossible to tell, really . . .). It's great for understanding your personality and, some say, for predicting the future. Historically many Chinese put a great deal of stock in this system, using it to name newborns, choose leaders, and arrange marriages.

The Chinese system is organized so that the year you were born in—not the month—determines your sign. (Oh, and remember, the Chinese year starts and ends around the beginning of February.)

Keep in mind that Chinese astrology is waaay more complicated than what we'll talk about here. Each sign has several different variations within it, based on what time of year and where in the world you were born. Which would explain why, even if your three best friends are all the same sign as you are, you don't all have the same exact personality.

Still, even the basics of the basics can give you some cool clues to who you are and some new things to think about.

Use this key to figure out your sign, as well as the signs of your friends and family, then read on!

If you were born in:

Then you are:

January 28, 1960-February 14, 1961,
February 15, 1972-February 2, 1973
February 2, 1984-February 19, 1985
February 19, 1996-February 6, 1997

A RAT

February 15, 1961-February 4, 1962
February 3, 1973-January 22, 1974
February 20, 1985-February 8, 1986
February 7, 1997-January 27, 1998

AN OX

February 5, 1962-January 24, 1963
January 23, 1974-February 10, 1975
February 9, 1986-January 28, 1987
January 28, 1998-February 15, 1999

A TIGER

January 25, 1963-February 12, 1964
February 11, 1975-January 30, 1976
January 29, 1987-February 16, 1988
February 16, 1999-February 4, 2000

A RABBIT

February 13, 1964-February 1, 1965
January 31, 1976-February 17, 1977
February 17, 1988-February 5, 1989
February 5, 2000-January 23, 2001

A DRAGON

February 2, 1965-January 20, 1966
February 18, 1977-February 6, 1978
February 6, 1989-January 26, 1990
January 24, 2001-February 11, 2002

A SNAKE

If you were born in:

Then you are:

January 21, 1966-February 8, 1967
February 7, 1978-January 27, 1979
January 27, 1990-February 14, 1991
February 12, 2002-January 31, 2003

A HORSE

February 9, 1967-January 29, 1968
January 28, 1979-February 15, 1980
February 15, 1991-February 3, 1992
February 1, 2003-January 21, 2004

A SHEEP

January 30, 1968-February 16, 1969
February 16, 1980-February 4, 1981
February 4, 1992-January 22, 1993
January 22, 2004-February 8, 2005

A MONKEY

February 17, 1969-February 5, 1970
February 5, 1981-January 24, 1982
January 23, 1993-February 9, 1994
February 9, 2005-January 28, 2006

A ROOSTER

February 6, 1970-January 26, 1971
January 25, 1982-February 12, 1983
February 10, 1994-January 20, 1995
January 29, 2006-February 17, 2007

A DOG

January 27, 1971-February 15, 1972
February 13, 1983-February 1, 1984
January 31, 1995-February 18, 1996
February 18, 2007-February 6, 2008

A BOAR

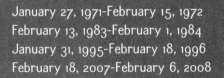

SO YOU'RE A RAT
Key word: *Resourceful*

The good deal: You're smart, crafty, and quick-thinking, and you *always* know what time it is. When people need answers, they come straight to you—after all, you're efficient and prompt, and you always have the 411 on the latest news, the wackest trivia, and the specials Taco Bell is running this week (no one likes to save a buck more than you do). As far as you're concerned, it's not a complete breakfast without all your vitamins, and it's not a complete day without some kind of plan or scheme. Nothing happens in your tight circle of friends that you don't know about . . . or participate in.

The bad deal: There's a serious gossip freak inside you, and if you don't zip it every now and then, your nosy self is gonna get in trouble.

Famous Rats
Ben Affleck
Gwyneth Paltrow
Shaquille O'Neal

You can be kind of cliquish, and when people aren't up to your standards, you can dis them pretty hard.

Your fashion sense: If it was on sale, you're probably wearing it.

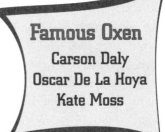

牛 SO YOU'RE AN OX

Key word: *Practical*

The good deal: You're the most reliable, patient, and helpful animal there is. Kindness is your middle name. If I needed someone to keep a secret, I'd call you. You've got an amazing sense of responsibility—and probably a perfect attendance record. Everyone knows where to find you the night before a math exam: hunched over your laptop, making sure you're prepared. You care about being as strong and healthy "as an ox"! Stamina is your other middle name, and you also love to spend time alone, so you'll probably go out running after reading this.

Famous Oxen
Carson Daly
Oscar De La Hoya
Kate Moss

The bad deal: Some people probably think you're a little narrow-minded, but really it's just that you're kind of stubborn. It takes a lot to piss you off, but when you're pissed, you stay that way for a long time. You're not the most romantic person around and often choose to use your head when others want you to use your heart.

Your fashion sense:
I bet you're wearing jeans.

SO YOU'RE A TIGER

Key word: *Intense*

The good deal: Stand back, y'all. We got a live one. This tiger is fearless, passionate, strong, and brave. Like I had to tell you that. You're restless sometimes, impulsive sometimes, and always funny as hell. People notice your dynamic spirit, and if there's a spotlight nearby, you'll jump into it. Can you say *charisma*? You are also incredibly romantic but in unusual ways—you'd rather give

your prom date a massage than a corsage. When people hang with you, you make them feel like they're the only one in your heart. Because they are. At least, at the moment.

Famous Tigers
Jewel
Leonardo DiCaprio
Eminem

The bad deal: All that energy can take you to good places or to bad ones . . . and your rebellious streak sometimes goes too far. You're daring, that's for sure, but you get annoyed when other, more sensible people aren't. It comes from being selfish. Oh, and then there's that temper. Man, if someone crosses you once, you can be sure they never will again.

Your fashion sense: Very unique. And probably very colorful.

SO YOU'RE A RABBIT

Key word: *Lucky*

The good deal: You're thoughtful, kind, energetic, open-minded, graceful, and you're probably gonna live a nice long life. Humor is essential to your happiness, but with your good sense of judgment and mature attitude, bathroom jokes just seem cheap and stupid to you. Sophistication is written all over your zit-free face. You love the arts, so it's not like you need a field trip to make it to the museum. As far as you're concerned, there's nothing in the universe better than peace, and you'll do anything to maintain it. And damn, you have good taste! (Oops, sorry, I cussed . . . you're not into that. My bad.)

Famous Rabbits
Drew Barrymore
Lauryn Hill
Tiger Woods

The bad deal: Who's the first to bolt when trouble comes around? You, dude. Yep, in your lifelong quest for peace and quiet, you sometimes blow things off when they get tough. Like sometimes you're more likely to dump a friend who's dissed you than to try and work it out. Smart? I think not.

Your fashion sense: It's all about comfort. You're a khaki.

SO YOU'RE A DRAGON

Key word: *Strong*

The good deal: You go. You go big. Then you go again. Yep, there's no stopping a dragon. Enthusiastic and a bag of chips, you'll try anything once and succeed. (And if you don't, so what? You could if you really wanted to.) You've got a charming side, and the limelight loves you—in fact, for everyone else's fifteen minutes of fame you'll clock an hour. (And if you need to breathe a little fire to make sure that spotlight keeps burning, well, why not?) You believe in yourself big time, and you always mean what you say, even if you change your mind a lot. You'll fight hard for what's right and fight hard against what's wrong. Sure, you might have a bit of a temper, but you'll forgive anyone anything.

The bad deal: You probably have no clue how intimidating you are, but know this: You have the ability to scare the crap out of people without even trying. Why? Because the other side of your enormous strength is . . . your enormous strength. *Bossy, overconfident,* and *inconsiderate* are what people probably whisper about you behind your back.

Famous Dragons

JC Chasez
Reese Witherspoon
Freddie Prinze, Jr.

Your fashion sense: You're a sharp dresser, but not trendy.

蛇 SO YOU'RE A SNAKE

Key word: *Wise*

The good deal: You're on a different wavelength from the rest of the world, thanks to your thoughtful intelligence, ambition, and obvious charisma (think about it—when's the last time anyone's been able to take their eyes off a snake?). You're kind of a mystery—smooth on the outside but obviously strong and even dangerous on the inside. People admire you. You're more psychic than any 970 wack could ever hope to be because you believe in your instinct and have great judgment about when to use it and when not to. You're magical but practical. Oh, and by the way, you are one sexy reptile, with outfits to match. Ouch!

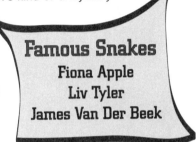

Famous Snakes
Fiona Apple
Liv Tyler
James Van Der Beek

The bad deal: Look up *shady* in the dictionary and you'll probably find a picture of the Snake. They made up that word just for you. You're evasive, private, and on occasion straight-up icy cold. And sometimes, when you've got the world believing you're lost in your own powerful thoughts, you're actually planning to strike the person who pissed you off last week. After all, as far as you're concerned, they deserve it.

Your fashion sense: Was that you bum rushing the runway at the latest fashion show to snag the looks off the models?

SO YOU'RE A HORSE
Key word: *Magnetic*

The good deal: You're the first to arrive at the party and the last to leave. (Unless there's a better party going on down the block, which you will know about and make it to.) Popular doesn't even begin to describe you—for you, your social life is a full-time job and no one in the world is nearly as good at it. You're funny, talkative, and open-minded. You love a challenge, even if you don't always follow through with it. You take pride in your decisiveness and independence. You love the outdoors and love to get physical (I'm talking about working out here, you perv!), and there's no parking on the dance floor when you're in the house. You are straight-up irresistible.

The bad deal: They made a movie of your life, and it's called *How to Be a Player*. You may or may not be a bona fide hoochie pop, but you're definitely a major flirt. You are moody (aren't you?), and you can be really harsh when you get mad, even with people you care about. And you probably talk on your cell phone during movies. How annoying.

Your fashion sense: Show-off. You've got the latest looks—in the brightest colors.

Famous Horses
Katie Holmes
Kobe Bryant
Aaliyah

SO YOU'RE A SHEEP

Key word: *Compassionate*

The good deal: You're gentle, honest, understanding, peaceful, and generous, and let's face it: People like you. They really, really like you. You like to take things at a slow and steady pace, and while some people think you're a slowpoke, you know that racing through life means missing some of the good stuff. Solo sports are totally your speed—running, biking, boxing, or swimming. You never forget a friend's birthday, you're an amazing listener, you're the ultimate shoulder to lean on, and no one you care about ever cries alone if you can help it. The rest of the world is incredibly lucky to have you around. And you're a straight-up, dyed-in-the-wool (get it? wool?) romantic at heart. Mushy, even.

Famous Sheep

Christina Ricci
Claire Danes
Gavin Rossdale

The bad deal: You set your own pace, and since it doesn't always mesh with everyone else's, you can feel isolated, lonely, and sometimes depressed. Unfortunately, it's not in your generally shy nature to speak up about it, so people have to pry it out of you, forcing you to say what's on your mind. People could get bored with this routine and eventually decide you're too high maintenance.

Your fashion sense: Your outfit is planned and perfect, from head to toe.

41

猴 SO YOU'RE A MONKEY

Key word: *Ingenious*

The good deal: They invented the word *inventive* especially for you, Monkey. You're quick, smart, funny, and curious. People count on you to crack a joke when it's desperately needed. You're on the social tip most of the time, and you bounce easily between cliques. You value your freedom, and whenever anyone tries to pin you down, you make a point of surprising them by changing course. One look, and you can see through almost anything and anyone—and put them right in their place. But even if you piss them off, you're never worried . . . you'll find a way to get back on their good side soon enough.

tucker says

I'm a Monkey. You can call me ingenious, inventive, quick, funny, and clever if you want to. Go ahead.

The bad deal: This "rules-are-made-for-breaking!" attitude of yours has definite backfire potential—every now and then you'll run into someone (probably a Tiger) who loses patience with you. Hey, you deserve it. You're easily tempted into risky, even dangerous behavior—and you're famous for always going one step too far. That insensitivity can really hurt people, you know.

Your fashion sense: Trendy. By the time Old Navy advertises it, you're already dropping it off at Goodwill.

SO YOU'RE A ROOSTER
Key word: *Alert*

The good deal: You care, deeply, about the world and everything (and everyone) in it. That's why you pay such close attention all the time. There's nothing you can't deal with head-on because you're prepared, careful, and very, very brave. You're the first one up in

Famous Roosters
Natalie Portman
Britney Spears
Heather Graham

the morning (cock-a-doodle-doo), you work hard, and you expect the same from others. No one gets to the heart of things faster than you do—your directness, decisiveness, and ability to deal in a crisis are legendary. You always finish your homework early because there's so much more stuff to take care of once you're done. You like a lot of positive feedback, and you get it because you deserve it.

The bad deal: It's never easy being a total perfectionist. Since there is no such thing as "perfect," you run the risk of constantly being disappointed, even when everyone else is satisfied. You don't always soften the blow when you deliver your famous reality checks, and people walk away much more wounded than you wanted them to be. Oh, and quit bragging about how on the ball you are, already. It's annoying.

Your fashion sense: Logos—the bigger and brighter, the better

狗 SO YOU'RE A DOG
Key word: *Loyal*

The good deal: You're totally likable, attractive, and playful. Not only that, you're a quick learner and you aim to please. Who wouldn't want you around? You know good from bad, and you always fall on the good side of things. You're the best friend imaginable—loyal, affectionate, and extremely protective. If anyone disses you or your posse, they'll feel your bite. But forgiveness is your specialty, and anyone who wants to meet you halfway will be surprised—you'll go even further. There's no secret you won't keep for a friend. Oh, and when things suck and there's bad news to be shared, you have a gift for making everything okay in the end.

Famous Dogs
Jennifer Lopez
Prince William
LeAnn Rimes

The bad deal: Sometimes being as loyal as you are can get you into trouble. When someone you trust does something stupid or cruel, you tend to ignore it—after all, how could someone you love so much do something so wrong? You have a tendency to snap when things don't go your way, and that sucks for whoever's responsible. And thanks to your sense of duty to your friends, you can get pretty judgmental about people who don't fit the mold.

Your fashion sense: Classic and simple. Your mama would be proud. In fact, she probably picked out your outfit. They invented the word *prep* for you.

SO YOU'RE A BOAR

Key words: *Heart of gold*

The good deal: You're generous, popular, quiet, honest, and sincere. To you, the greatest happiness is when everyone around you is getting along perfectly. Your friends can expect love from you today, tomorrow, and forever—you, more than any other sign, are awesome at keeping up lifelong friendships. Anyone who's ever asked you for help knows you'll go out of your way to lend a hand, and you have no kind of problem making and keeping commitments. You might seem like a bit of a loner, but really you're just soulful and deep.

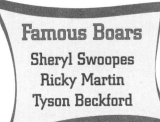

Famous Boars

Sheryl Swoopes
Ricky Martin
Tyson Beckford

The bad deal: No one would ever guess, but you have a tendency to overdo it. What's your pleasure? Video games? Potato chips? Shopping? Whatever your weakness, you love to indulge it, sometimes too much. You're kind of naive sometimes and tend to let people really take advantage of your kindness. Oh, and just because your casa is our casa doesn't necessarily mean we all feel the same way—you gotta ask before you move in on our stuff.

Your fashion sense: You borrowed that outfit, didn't you?

Check page 156 for where to find out more about Chinese astrology.

your BRAIN

RIGHT BRAIN

- INTUITION
- VISUAL THINKING
- EMOTIONS
- MUSIC
- SENSUALITY

LEFT BRAIN

- LOGIC
- REASON
- NUMBERS
- WORDS
- ANALYSIS

are you a
RIGHTY OR A LEFTY?
(BRAIN, THAT IS . . .)

SO WE ALL KNOW THAT THE BRAIN IS DIVIDED into two parts, right? And the left half of your brain controls the right half of your body, and the right half of your brain controls the left half of your body, right? Right. But wait, there's more. Research shows that the two halves of the brain are responsible for more than different sides of your body—they're also in charge of different kinds of thinking.

The left brain is more about logic, reason, numbers, words, and analyzing information.

The right brain is more about intuition, visual thinking, emotions, music, and sensuality.

We all use both sides of our brain all the time, and it's a good thing we do because we desperately need them both. Still, most of us seem to favor one side over the other.

Check out the next few pages to find out which side *you* use the most.

THE TEST

CHOOSE A OR B.

1. You drive by a car accident. You:

A. *Wonder about the details. How fast were the cars going? Who hit who?*

B. *Worry about the people involved. Are they okay? Are their families going to freak?*

2. It's 9 P.M. You switch the TV to:

A. *Some game show.*

B. *Some nighttime soap.*

3. Computers are great for:

A. *Taking care of business.*

B. *Creating cool Web pages.*

4. Which do you trust more?

A. *The facts.*

B. *Your gut feelings.*

5. To you, an unfinished jigsaw puzzle is:

A. *Inviting, and you'll sit down to finish it.*

B. *Annoying, and you'll ignore it.*

6. The best part about acing an exam is:

A. *Beefing up your academic record.*

B. *Feeling a sense of achievement.*

7. Your best friend comes to you with a big problem. You:

A. *Try to solve it right away.*

B. *Hold her hand and listen sympathetically.*

YOUR RESULTS

If you chose more A answers than B answers, you use your left brain more. If you chose more B answers than A answers, you use your right brain more. If you're about evenly split, you use them both. (Or you're using neither one, you slacker.)

LEFT BRAIN KEY WORDS	RIGHT BRAIN KEY WORDS
Verbal communication	Body language
Facts	Intuition
1 + 1 = 2	1 + 1 = a relationship
Intellect	Emotion
Math and science	Art and music
Freeway	Back roads
Discovery Channel	MTV
Realist	Idealist
Sympathetic	Empathetic

Most people feel more comfortable identifying with one or the other, but we all know you need to balance both to be complete. Like, you can't play all day at the amusement park unless you work for some cash first. Or you can't have a solid relationship unless you're willing to have a fight every now and then. But that's what makes life interesting—things shift constantly, and we always have to adapt.

tucker says

Yesterday I took this quiz and determined I was a right brain dude. Then this afternoon I took it again and found myself solidly in the left brain camp. What does this tell me? Well, like I said before, two halves or not, it's still one brain up there. And like everyone else, I have to use the whole thing to get by. Sometimes left, sometimes right, always thinking.

Check page 157 for where to find out more about left brain/right brain.

your *native american clan*

what's your
native american clan?

IT'S BEEN ESTIMATED THAT THERE WERE OVER
five hundred Native American nations in North America before
Columbus showed up half a millennium ago. The fact is, now we
know that there were a whole lot more than that. And each nation
was distinct, unique, complex, and important. But one characteristic
shared by nearly all of them, from the Inuit of the far North to the
Hopi of the desert Southwest, was a complete, all-important connection to nature and the environment. Especially the sky.

Much like astrologists all over the planet, Native American groups
used the skies to attempt to make sense of who they were and what
their purpose was. They paid close attention to the changing seasons,
the shifting forces in nature, and the constellations to figure it all out.

Over the last thirty years a collective of Native American
scholars and spiritual guides in the Northwest have compiled some
of the most common elements of over twenty thousand ancient traditions to create a modern version of Native American astrology
using birth dates to divide people into "clans." All of us, Native
American or not, can use this system to better understand ourselves
and our relation to nature.

Find your birthday to figure out what clan you're in, then read up:

If you were born:
December 22-January 19, the time of the **snow goose**
April 20-May 20, the time of the **beaver**
August 23-September 22, the time of the **brown bear**

then you are a member of the *Turtle Clan.*

If you were born:
January 20-February 18, the time of the **otter**
May 21-June 20, the time of the **deer**
September 23-October 23, the time of the **raven**

then you are a member of the *Butterfly Clan.*

If you were born:
February 19-March 20, the time of the **cougar**
June 21-July 22, the time of the **flicker fish**
October 24-November 21, the time of the **snake**

then you are a member of the *Frog Clan.*

If you were born:
March 21-April 19, the time of the **red hawk**
July 23-August 22, the time of the **sturgeon**
November 22-December 21, the time of the **elk**

then you are a member of the *Thunderbird Clan.*

The Turtle Clan

Your colors: Brown, leaf green, deep blue, violet
You rule because: You're solid, dependable, and strong.
But sometimes: You're inflexible.

about you:

Face it. You walk into a room, and people smile. Is it because you arrived on time? Or because you have the kind of energy that makes everyone trust you right up front? Probably both. You're always dependable, you do what you say you're going to do, and you keep all promises—and secrets. Your keep-it-real attitude keeps everyone else in check. And best of all, your confidence and your belief in yourself inspire people instead of intimidating them.

your gift: perseverance

Once you start something, you don't stop until you get it done to your satisfaction. And you've got the strength and willpower to do it. You'll focus on a goal completely until you reach it, and you'll plow through obstacles—especially people who say you "can't"—like they don't even exist. When others around you are busy discussing how to solve a problem, you've already knocked it down and moved on (partly because you're a multitasking master).

how you relate:

You *love* people. Not that you're Señor or Señorita Popular, necessarily, but you really dig all kinds of people—you think everyone's got a story to tell. You have the kind of vibe that makes people want to sit, chill, talk, and just hang. But your tradition-al, steady personality sometimes keeps you from sharing your own story, which sometimes leaves people thinking you're a little chilly.

your struggle: perfectionism

It's not the easiest thing in the world to be so good at what you do. It makes you expect everyone to be up to your standards. But the thing is, not even *you* are up to your standards all the time. You expect perfection, but the fact is (and you learned this in kindergarten), there's no such thing as perfect. Not that you should lower your standards, but you might want to raise your forgiveness level—in relation to others and yourself.

The Butterfly Clan

Your colors: Clear, silver, light green, sand
You rule because: You're open-minded, adaptable, and unpredictable.
But sometimes: You're indecisive.

about you:

Like a butterfly, you're able to go with the flow of life, to ride the wind and deal with wherever it takes you—looking great the whole way. You're better than anyone else at handling change (after all, you were once a caterpillar), thanks to plenty of energy, optimism, and creativity. Your roots are superimportant to you, and you're able to hang on to them—even when your world is in full-on wack mode.

your gift: communication

You're an amazing, creative communicator—not just because you're so articulate but because you always have an intuitive sense of *who* you're talking to and what to say to make them understand. People love having you around because you're able to make sense of things that confuse everyone else. You not only tell people that things matter—you show them *how* they matter. And you don't say much that doesn't involve a little humor—you've got the gift of laughter, which infects everyone around you.

how you relate:

People always want to hang with you, especially when they're stressed—everyone knows how soothing a butterfly can be. They admire with your open-mindedness and ability to go with the flow. And they love the way you show everyone how beautiful and talented they are, no matter who they are.

People get frustrated with you, though, because you change your mind all the time. Your amazing ability to roll with life's punches means you're a survivor, but it also means rethinking your point of view constantly. Easy for you to do, but not easy for everyone else to understand. Luckily you've got that gift for communication—use it, and everyone will be up-to-date on where you're fluttering next.

your struggle: self-awareness

Your biggest struggle in life will be to stay grounded—you move so easily from one situation to the next that sometimes it's difficult to keep in mind what's truly important to you. Try to remember: As much as you change and grow from day to day, you're still the same person you were yesterday.

The Frog Clan

Your colors: Blue-green, pink, copper
You rule because: You're empathetic, intuitive, and inspiring.
But sometimes: You're a drama queen/king.

about you:

Ain't nothing you can't bounce back from, Frog. You can take anything that life tosses at you and make your way through it. And not only that, if life isn't tossing you what you need, you'll find a way to get it, anyway. But what's most amazing about you is your ability to *feel* everything so deeply. You're a member of the most emotional clan, which some people perceive as weak—until you show them that your emotions, and your ability to work through them, make you stronger.

your gift: intuition

You can size up a situation and everyone in it with little more than a quick glance. Others rely on facts and logic, and you see the value in that, too—but for you, there's more. Your gut fills you in on a lot of the details. Sure, you check the scoreboard just like everyone else at the basketball game, but you seem to know somehow who's gonna win just by watching the players.

how you relate:

You're practically psychic, the way you're able to understand what people are going through. Just a quick glance at your best friend on Friday night and you know immediately whether to rev up for a party or for a late night coffee talk at Denny's. You love to share your emotions with others, and you especially love it when they share theirs back. You love to touch people, literally and emotionally. Making connections matters to you. You believe that everything, *everything*, matters.

On the bummer side, your desire to understand others and help them out sometimes makes you, well, a little nosy. See, some people don't feel as comfortable sharing their deepest and darkest as you do, especially if they don't know you all that well. And hey! That's okay. Got it?

your struggle: **emotional balance**

So you laugh when it's funny and cry when it's sad! What's the big deal? Well, it isn't a big deal. In fact, it could be considered your other gift. But sometimes your emotions get in the way of your ability to cope. Learning to keep things in perspective will take you far.

The Thunderbird Clan

Your colors: Red, yellow, black
You rule because: You're energetic, innovative, and charming.
But sometimes: You burn out.

about you:

You're first in line, a pioneer, maybe even a rebel. You don't think stuff—you do stuff. As in, who cares if I don't have a backpack; sign me up for the hundred-mile walk-a-thon! As in, screw the fact that I have a midterm tomorrow—let's party tonight! Luckily you're quick, clever, and inventive

tucker says

I'm in the Thunderbird clan. It's all true. Except for the part about being on the list. Can I get on the list already?

enough to pull it off, most of the time. Besides, living is more important than planning, right? And damn, why'd you have to be such a hottie?

your gift: innovation

You can do almost anything, and you can fake anything you can't do well enough until you learn. Which you always do, quickly. When people need a problem solved, they turn to you—because they know you'll come up with a solution they'd never have thought of. You also love to experiment—you're always looking for a new route to school, or flipping to a new radio station. And the more you experiment, the more innovative you become.

how you relate:

You're on the list, dawg. Yep, you're charming and magnetic, and everyone wants you—not just at their party but on their team and at their dinner table. Okay, and most of them want to make out with you, too. Optimism and enthusiasm are what you're all about, especially when you're truly, madly, deeply psyched about something.

But along with your enthusiasm comes a, uh, sometimes overpowering nature. Not to mention a tendency to be a little hot and cold. The Thunderbird is associated with the element of fire, which, while it's warming and nurturing is also overwhelming, sometimes destructive to people, and eventually burns out until it's lit again. Kind of like, well, you.

your struggle: patience

Things just don't move quickly enough for you, sometimes . . . do they? As far as you're concerned, time spent planning, or waiting, or remembering is time wasted. But the thing is, it's not all about everything that's going on out there. Take a minute to check out what's going on in your head.

Check page 157 for where to find out more about Native American Clans.

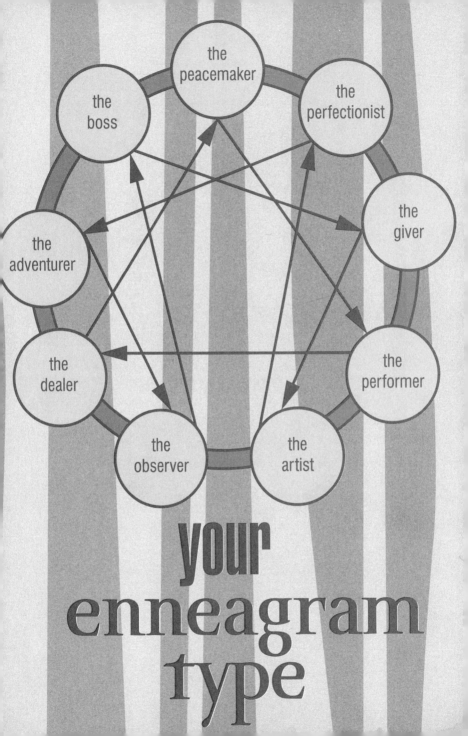

your
enneagram
type

what's your
enneagram type?

NO ONE KNOWS EXACTLY WHO CAME UP WITH
the Enneagram or where or when the idea originated. We *do* know
it gained popularity several thousand years ago in western or cen-
tral Asia (somewhere near modern-day Syria, Turkey, or Iraq)
before fading into obscurity. It was revived by Sufi Muslim mystics
about six hundred years ago. Since then all kinds of people have
studied it and refined it.

Believe it or not, all the mystery surrounding the Enneagram's
beginnings only makes it more legit in the eyes of its fans—they
believe that since it's survived so long under such mysterious circum-
stances, well, there must really be something to it.

But what exactly is the Enneagram? It's a way of putting different types of people onto a sort of graph, making it easier to recognize characteristics of each type and understand how different
types are similar and different. The system, based on nine types that
move and flow into each other, is usually shown as a nine-pointed
geometric shape. (See? Over there on page 59? That's what it
looks like.)

Each point on the Enneagram represents a personality type, and

the lines connecting the points represent the most common ways people's personalities develop from one type to the next. Sometimes moving between the points represents positive growth; sometimes it represents backtracking.

Most Enneagram experts believe that we each have all nine types within us but one is most dominant at any particular point in our lives. Like, even though you have all nine types in you, one of them, say, the Helper, might be dominant for a period of your life. Then maybe the Boss might become more dominant, and then the Adventurer. See, the people who developed this system understood that we all change a lot, even during a single day.

The Enneagram is incredibly complex, and people spend their entire lives studying it. Which is awesome for them. But I'm sticking to the tip of the iceberg tip here because that's all it takes to get your brain flowing.

So, flow. Take the little quiz on the next few pages to help find your spot on the Enneagram. Answer the questions by picking the answer that *best* describes you (you have to choose one answer even if more than one seems to fit). Then check out your results.

1. What matters most to you today?

A. Perfection

B. Helping others

C. Feedback from others

D. Being unique

E. Learning

F. Your sense of duty

G. Fun

H. Strength

I. Peace

2. When you were a kid, you:

A. Always wanted to be the best.

B. Worried a lot about others.

C. Always tried to get noticed.

D. Spent lots of time alone.

E. Read a lot of books.

F. Always behaved yourself.

G. Were always getting into trouble.

H. Were always in charge.

I. Avoided fights.

3. Which best describes you? Be honest.

A. I like things done my way.

B. I have a hard time saying no to people.

C. I'm a show-off.

D. Happy people annoy me, even when I'm happy.

E. I don't like sharing my feelings.

F. I take care of business.

- G. I love making plans, but I hate keeping them.

H. I refuse to be told what to do.

I. I don't mind letting others have their way, even if I don't get mine.

4. Your best friend scores 100% on her French exam. How do you feel about it?

A. So what? So did I!

B. I oughta buy her a soda or something.

C. I went to France once! I ate croissants. Cool, huh?

D. French is such a cool-sounding language. Wait, who scored what?

E. Cool! I wonder how she studied.

F. I hope she doesn't screw up the grade curve.

G. That's great. Now let's go scope some hotties!

H. Who cares? French is stupid. She should be taking Spanish instead.

- I. That's nice! I hope she doesn't ask me what I got.

5. You're shopping for shoes. How do you decide on a pair?

A. They have to fit exactly right. And match that denim outfit.

B. I'll get the cheap ones, then get something for my sister.

C. A little pizzazz never hurt anyone!

D. If I've never seen them on anyone else, they're mine.

E. I read about these kicks in a magazine, and I'm hunting for them. And only them.

F. What's here, and what fits?

G. Look, these shoes need to take me from beach to mountaintop and from day to evening.

H. All I know is they better not cost too much.

I. My shoes need to go with everything in my closet.

6. What's the key to getting along with you?

A. Show up on time.

B. Be nice to me and everyone else.

C. Pay attention to me, a lot.

D. Leave me alone sometimes!

E. Teach me something new.

F. Roll with me. Be flexible.

G. Be up for anything!

H. Let me have my way.

I. No fighting!

7. When you're bored, you:

A. Clean your room. Again.

B. Call your grandmother, just for the heck of it.

C. Start calling all your friends.

D. Put on your headphones and jam out.

E. Check out a couple of Web sites you've never been to.

F. Finish your homework.

G. Bored? Who's bored?

H. Start making plans involving other people. With or without telling them.

I. Feel thankful to have a moment of peace.

your results

Okay, let's keep it simple, shall we?

If most of the statements you picked are: then you're probably:

A's . . . . the Perfectionist

B's . . . . the Giver

C's . . . . the Performer

4 D's . . . . the Artist

7 E's . . . . the Observer

3 F's . . . . the Dealer

2 G's . . . . the Adventurer

H's . . . . the Boss

I's . . . . the Peacemaker

If you have a tie, read the results for both types.

theperfectionist

you're cool because: You're self-disciplined, conscientious, reliable, and realistic.
you're annoying because: You're judgmental.

the upside:

Want things done right? Ask a Perfectionist. Yep, you Perfectionists always know, intuitively, how things should be done. You can tell the difference between black and white in an instant, even when everyone else just sees gray. You're productive, and you know you drive your lab partner crazy with details. You're very realistic, and you never say you'll do anything unless you know you can do it perfectly. You Perfectionists are honest because that's the *right* way to be, and you always apologize when you blow it. Oh, and you expect the same from everyone else, too. So they best shape up.

the downside:

You know you can go a little overboard trying to make things perfect all the time (in fact, you probably went through the questions for this section two or three times), then you probably get mad at yourself for being so anal. And you have a difficult time making decisions because you focus on what might go wrong instead of what might go right. Perfectionists can be very judgmental and critical of others, and face it, you can be annoyingly preachy sometimes.

your career:

Most Perfectionists choose careers where they know, exactly, when they're being perfect. You know, careers in hard science, where you know for sure when you're right or wrong. Or banking. Or managing other people. You can run a small business, too, if you give yourself a break and let stuff slide every now and then.

thegiver

you're cool because: You're compassionate, generous, funny, and very kind.
you're annoying because: You're needy.

the upside:

You're nice, warm, and the kind of person people come to for a major hug—and the cookies and milk to go with it. You might not solve their problems, but you'll sure make them *feel* better. You're extremely supportive of others, and you show it not just by patting them on the back but by getting your hands dirty to be helpful however you can. Humor is majorly important to you—and you know even dirty jokes feed the soul if they make you laugh. Incredibly loyal, no matter what, you'll always stick up for your friends and family . . . maybe even more than you stick up for yourself.

the downside:

All this give, give, give can get to you after a while. How about a little take, take, take? Fact is, not everyone appreciates you as much as they should, and it pisses you off every now and then. Right? Even though you'd never really complain about it, you'll let them know in your own way—maybe by copping a guilt trip or working the silent treatment. You have a hard time saying no, and you feel really bad about yourself when you think you haven't done enough . . . even when you have.

your career:

You'd rule as a teacher. You're awesome with kids, which means you'd also be a great parent. The health and medical world could use you, big time—a dose of your compassion and empathy sure wouldn't hurt them. Anywhere you get to help people out—as a realtor, helping them find a home; as a counselor or therapist, helping them cope; or as a consultant, helping them solve problems—is a good place for you to be.

theperformer

you're cool because: You're self-confident, adaptable, and lively. You're an overachiever.
you're annoying because: You're vain.

the upside:

Who's that fine-looking specimen with the dope threads? That's you, Performer, and by the way, nice job on that last exam you aced. You've been working hard, and it's showing. Optimism is your middle name—even when you're in the middle of a major setback, it's not hard for you to see the light at the end of the tunnel. You're efficient, informed, outgoing, and friendly. Your speed dial has numbers for, well, everyone. Good thing, too, because you never know when you'll feel like throwing a house party at the drop of a hat.

the downside:

Hey, show-off! Sit down already! Jeez. Enough about you. Okay, maybe that's harsh, but your need for constant attention can really exhaust the rest of us. You've been known to spread your share of gossip, especially if it involves dissing someone you're feeling competitive with. Oh, and you probably spend way too much time in front of the mirror and way too much cash on face and hair products. There's more to life than looks.

your career:

Ambition is what gets you up in the morning and what keeps you awake at night—every day is an opportunity for you to get ahead. That means no matter what you choose to do with your life (and chances are, you'll have lots of careers), you won't stop until you hit the ceiling or break through it. Fast-track industries like technology, investing, publishing, and TV would love you.

theartist

you're cool because: You're creative, expressive, romantic, and colorful.
you're annoying because: You're moody.

the upside:

Each of you Artists is truly one of a kind . . . so much so that it's hard to write about all of you in a single paragraph. But I will. You guys sure experience things intensely—you're screaming with joy when the season premiere of *The Simpsons* comes on, then you're bawling your eyes out at the sappy Kodak commercial they play during the show. But you recognize that your feelings, whether happy or sad, are important parts of being human. What's more, you love to share these feelings with others, and no one knows how to do it better. Your world is a work in progress—it needs constant effort and improvement. Your job? To interpret it, in whatever way works best for you.

the downside:

Sure, you feel. That's a good thing. But you've been known to be down for weeks because of a sad piece of news you caught on television. It would be one thing if you felt things like that enough to do something about them, but you tend to feel them so deeply that you get paralyzed. Not that you tend to overreact or anything (note to everyone else: Don't ever tell Artists that they're overreacting . . . they'll stop listening), but sometimes things have an impact on you that goes beyond healthy, holding you back when you know you should be moving forward.

your career:

If you've got the raw talent and even rawer ambition to go with your Artist self, you could make a living in the arts, as a performer, director, designer, painter, rock star, writer, whatever. Spotlight make you sweat? Stick behind the scenes. Also, you'd make a kick-butt chef because you'd truly put your heart into it.

theobserver

you're cool because: You're original, perceptive, and well-spoken. You're a visionary.
you're annoying because: You're detached.

the upside:

You know the person who always knows exactly what to say at exactly the right time? Oh, of course you do—it's you. You've got a real talent for understanding a situation and putting your thoughts into words that everyone can relate to. You're very independent, and you're never afraid to state your opinion if you feel like it. You're clear about your ideas, and you know they'll constantly change as your wide-open-minded self goes through life. Some people call you opinionated, but then again, you never ask others to conform to your opinions. You have a few close friends, not a lot of semifriends. You ask questions because you want to know the answers, not because you want to hear yourself talk. And your perceptive little brain never misses a thing.

the downside:

The world doesn't always trust private people like you. Sure, you need a lot of time to yourself, but it's important for other people to know what's up with you—they happen to care about what's going on in your life. But after a while they'll will stop being intrigued by your mysteriousness and start getting bored with all the one-sided conversations. Shape up and start sharing. Oh, and how about a smile? There ya go.

your career:

Fire up the laptop because it's all about a career in information and communication for you. You've got a gift for breaking things down and making them mean something to other people. You can analyze anything down to the basics, so you'd rule in science and technology. Just be sure to choose a career that lets you work alone a lot . . . you need that.

the**dealer**

(as in, the One Who Can Deal with Anything)

you're cool because: You're warm, trusting, and brave.
You are a trooper.
you're annoying because: You're paranoid.

the upside:

Rain? Sigh. Earthquake? Whatever. Everything turning upside down all at once? Don't panic; don't worry. *You can deal.* You can deal because you're the Dealer. No matter what life throws at you, you always do what you need to do. You're very practical, not just in taking care of your own business but in helping others out, too. It's hard to pin you down sometimes because you keep yourself so busy . . . team sports, job, extracurriculars, hanging with friends. You love to participate, to belong, and you love group activity. In your world friendships rule. Oh, and you happen to be incredibly brave.

the downside:

It's true, you have a knack for confronting your fears, but that's because you've had a lot of practice; you've had a whole lot of fears to face. Your tendency to be pessimistic, defensive, and fearful is something your friends and family are well aware of. Insecurity sometimes keeps you out of the loop, and fear of failure sometimes keeps you from trying new things. Occasionally you get a little sarcastic about the world . . . "life sucks" is probably one of your favorite sayings, but at the end of the day you don't really believe it. Do you?

your career:

Ten-hut! You're smart enough, prepared enough, disciplined enough, tough enough, and group friendly enough to make it to the top of the ranks in law enforcement or the military. You'd be great in education—not only as a teacher but as an administrator or as a counselor, and you'd make a terrific lawyer.

theadventurer

you're cool because: You're spontaneous, talented, exciting, and charming.
you're annoying because: You're unreliable.

the upside:

If it's fun, you'll try it. If it's interesting, you'll investigate it. If it's food, you'll eat it. If it feels good, you'll do it. If it's one of the finer things in life, you *know* you love it. You are the first in line for everything, but you probably had to cut in to get there because standing in line is, well, no fun. People want you at their parties because your hearty go-for-it attitude is infectious. You get a lot done because you work at it. You have a free spirit, but you also value relationships. You need to be stimulated all the time or *bam*! You're off on another adventure.

the downside:

You're speeding through life, wringing every last drop of fun out of it, but the sad fact is, most people just can't keep up with you. They say you're impulsive and irresponsible; you say you're spontaneous and enthusiastic. Sure, people like you—you're way too charming not to like—but a deeper closeness? That takes effort, commitment, and patience—all within your reach if you really try. Another problem? Your grass-is-greener-over-there attitude doesn't always work, ya know. Oh, and if you paid attention in class every now and then, you might actually learn something.

your career:

If there's ever been an entrepreneur on the planet, it's you. You've got enthusiasm, imagination, energy, and confidence to spare, which means you should be able to conceive and build any kind of business—from software design to Vietnamese specialty foods—and score big. Whatever you do, make sure you get to move around a lot, advance quickly, and face new challenges every day, or you'll be out of there, fast.

the**boss**

you're cool because: You're direct, energetic, and self-confident. You're a leader.
you're annoying because: You're bossy.

the upside:

Ask anyone what they think of you, and odds are they'll spit out "confident" before you even finish the question. Yep, you're in charge of yourself and frequently in charge of others—in fact, you may even have your own family following your orders every now and then. You use your instinct to make snap decisions others agonize over forever. You're loyal and forgiving . . . and you believe strongly in following a life plan: Marriage and children are very important to you. Bosses are role models, even to people they don't know, and when you speak, people really do pay attention.

the downside:

Enough with bossing people around all the time. Just because you act like you're important doesn't mean you get to call *all* the shots. People get to make their own decisions every now and then. You can be domineering, taking over a room when you walk in, sometimes without even noticing it. Some people say you're aggressive (you'd call it assertive), some say you're insensitive (you'd call it honest), some say you're a control freak (hey, that's going a little far . . .). You're skeptical of plans that aren't your own, even if you suspect they might be better than yours.

your career:

Hi, did you notice the name of this type? It's called the Boss. That's you, sport. It doesn't matter what you choose to do—you'll end up a leader because of your decisiveness, your ability to solve problems, and your amazing ability to get people excited about stuff. Oh, and you'll have the guts to fire the suckers who just aren't up to your standards. How do *you* spell C-E-O?

thepeacemaker

you're cool because: You're peaceful, open-minded, generous, and patient.

you're annoying because: You're a flake.

the upside:

You've got a jones to increase the peace in this world, and you *define* calm, cool, and collected. People love to hang with you when they're stressed out or exhausted because your relax-everything's-going-to-be-fine point of view is exactly the message they need to hear. Got a fight going on in your group of friends? You're the one to solve it, you li'l diplomat, you. You never ask anyone to justify themselves because being judgmental is completely impossible for you. You live and let live. Face it, Peacemaker: When they came up with the saying "go with the flow," they were talking about you. Peace!

the downside:

Wake up, Peacemaker—if you want to make it anywhere in this world, you're actually going to have to make a little effort every now and then. That's right—good things happen because people *make* them happen. You've got this notion that if you wait long enough, happy things will fall in your lap (hey, they do), but don't you sometimes want to choose those happy things yourself? People get frustrated with you sometimes because even though they can count on you to be chill, they can't count on you to be on time or energetic. They want to call you a big old bump on a log, but they know if they did, you'd just ignore them, anyway.

your career:

Conflicts? No problem. You can solve any interpersonal war because you're the only personality type that can listen intently and deeply enough to really get to the heart of the problem. That's why you could find yourself commuting to the UN building every morning—and eventually taking over the ambassadorship of a foreign country. And if international living isn't for you, check out psychiatry, teaching, or even tarot reading—anything where you're helping people out.

tucker says

So, I know you're dying to know, what am I? Well, generally I'm the Observer, but sometimes I find myself solidly (and happily) in the Peacemaker camp. And when the pressure's on, I look a whole lot like a Performer. Confused? I'm not—after all, the Enneagram is all about moving around the grid. No one is locked into one type forever.

Check page 156 for where to find out more about the Enneagram.

your *inner* *goddess*

who's your inner goddess?

SO ALONG ABOUT THE END OF LAST CENTURY
sometime, these two shrinks named Jennifer and Roger Woolger
(yep, they're married) came up with a way for people to identify
what's most important to them, what drives their personalities, and
how they deal with the world. They used six powerful goddesses
from ancient Greece as examples of each type, figuring that everyone could identify with one or more of the six. (*Everyone*. That
includes you, fellas. Go ahead, get in touch with your feminine side.
And if that's just too much to ask, check this section for the kind of
girl you're interested in.)

The Woolgers' theories were very complex and deep, but luckily they broke it down into the easy-to-understand Goddess Wheel.
Read about all of the Goddesses, then ask yourself, which one is
most like you?

Athena

the goddess of wisdom and civilization

Key words: *intellect, education, justice, cities*

What you're like: Athena, you're focused on achievement. You're very bright, but also mad disciplined. You work hard (you always have *sooo* much work to do!), and you turn everything in on time and complete, no matter what it takes. Whatever you do after school (a job, extracurriculars, whatever) is something you're doing with an eye toward the future— you know it'll help beef up your college applications. College, and the rest of your life, will probably be in a big city because Athena, you like urban living. Oh, and you're into technology big time—whenever there's a PalmPilot upgrade, you're first in line.

Aphrodite

the goddess of love and beauty

Key words: *romance, sexuality, art, music, relationships*

What you're like: Show me an Aphrodite girl and I'll show you a girl who always has a boyfriend. It just might not be the same boyfriend from one week to the next. See, Aphrodite, you're very in touch with your feelings about the opposite sex (or the same sex, if you're so inclined), and you can flirt with the best of them. Not to mention the fact that you look good *every single day* because appearance really matters to you. Guys are all over you, and no one knows how to deal with them better than you do. One day you'll probably inspire the painter or poet in your life (maybe even one or two you don't know about) to create a picture or write a song about you. cool.

Persephone
the goddess of the underworld

Key words: *spirituality, mysticism, healing, dreams*

What you're like: Although you may be a full-on New Age crystal worshiper, you, Persephone, are more likely to be just a regular person with very strong intuition and insight. You might be very religious, or you might not be, but you're definitely interested in spirituality and big questions about the meaning of life. You dream a lot, and you talk about your dreams a lot. (And if you don't, you should.) People always come to you when they get dumped because no one can heal a spirit and make someone feel better faster than you can—you're an awesome shoulder to cry on. Sometimes you might look or sound like you're a little out of it, but really you're thinking some pretty deep thoughts. For instance, you could be thinking about the Goddess Wheel because you understand it on a level everyone else just doesn't.

Artemis
the goddess of nature

Key words: *instinct, outdoors, athletics, animals*

What you're like: Who's that chick running naked through the forest? That's you, Artemis, and don't worry—you're not a freak. You just really love the outdoors. Fresh air is like food to you—without it, you might as well be starving. Artemis people identify with truly wild nature, wild animals, weather, and everything about the world that has nothing to do with people. You live through your body more than your mind—you like to *feel* things, not just know about them. During the summer you're never inside. You're the one who walks right up to the scariest dog in creation, scratches him behind the ears, and makes an instant friend. You're a true healer—but your concern is healing the body, not the spirit.

tucker says
I'm an Aphrodite because I'm such a hottie. Just kidding. The truth is, I'm a straight-up Artemis. Okay, with maybe a little Athena poking out of my head. Get it? Ha ha.

Demeter
the goddess of fertility and motherhood

Key words: *nurturing, reproduction, farming, and children*
What you're like: You're the one who's always making sure everyone's had enough to eat, the one who just loooooooooooves babies, the

one who's always giving out hugs. Demeter people like you are very in touch with kids of all ages, including grown-up ones. You want to make sure everyone's got the basics (food, shelter, and love) all the time. You're good at putting first things first, knowing that no one can climb a mountain or build a city or write a term paper without a well-balanced meal and a hug. You'll probably grow up to be a fantastic parent. Demeter is also the goddess of cultivation and the harvest, so you probably put together a killer Thanksgiving dinner.

Hera
the goddess of power

Key words: *leadership, rules and regulations, tradition, power*

What you're like: Hera girls love to run the show. Whether you're the president of the student council or the lead singer in a band, you're very concerned about what's right and what's wrong and which side everyone is on. You can be bossy sometimes, but only because you believe in rules and tradition. You're also very family oriented, Hera—to you, family relationships are by far the most important in life.

Check page 156 for where to find out more about the Goddess Wheel.

INTROVERT

SENSOR

extrovert

INTUITIVE

your
psychological profile

Perceiver

feeler

Judger

what's your
psychological profile?

SOME PEOPLE RELY ON ANCIENT TRADITIONS
like numerology or astrology to understand personalities. And some
people like to stick to science. For them psychology, psychiatry, and
anatomy are the *real* keys to understanding identity. If you're one of
these people, this chapter is right up your alley.

The most famous psychological profiling system (say that three
times fast) is the Myers-Briggs Type Indicator® (try saying *that* three
times fast). The experts who came up with it in the 1940s and 1950s
figured that anyone's personality could be understood based on
their answers to four basic questions: (1) Where do you draw your
energy from? (2) How do you take in information? (3) How do you
make decisions? and (4) How do you like to run your life? Each
question can be answered in two ways, and when all is said and
done, how you answer each question helps determine who you are.

So whataya say? Shall we give it a shot? Read on. When you're
done with this section, you'll understand the basics of the system
and, more important, some basic stuff about yourself.

extrovertsvs.introvert

This part of your personality is all about where you get your energy and inspiration. Do you find it within? Or without? It has a lot to do with how you deal with the people around you. Are you social? Are you a loner? Are you somewhere in between? Do you like to share your life with others? Are you content keeping to yourself?

In each row pick the word or phrase that best describes you. Yes, you have to pick the one that best describes you even if you relate to them both or don't relate to either one. Sorry. Tough. Keep track of how many you select from column a and how many you select from column b.

a	b
1. Popular	Loner
2. Party hearty	VCR and ice cream
3. Busy weekends	Relaxing weekends
4. Study group	Independent study
5. Bored being alone	Like time alone
6. Onstage	In the audience
7. Telephone chat	On-line chat
8. Action	Thought
9. Talk first	Think first
10. Wound up	Peaceful
11. Lots of friends	A few close friends

If you picked more from column a than column b, you are probably an Extrovert. If you picked more from column b, you are probably an Introvert.

if you're an *extrovert,* you probably:

- Think out loud.
- Look for inspiration from other people or from the world beyond your head.
- Have many friends and like making new friends.
- Love it when people call or stop by.
- Find big, crazy parties energizing, not overwhelming.
- Love to help people out, even if they don't ask.
- Love to share all your news with all your friends—things don't feel real until you share them.
- Need positive feedback from people—until someone else believes in you, it's hard for you to believe in yourself.
- Are always on the go.
- Are almost never alone except in the shower (sometimes).
- Talk during the movie.

if you're an *introvert,* you probably:

- Think first, talk later.
- Look for inspiration within yourself.
- Have a few close friends, who you'll keep forever.
- Get a little annoyed when you're interrupted by a phone call.
- Get exhausted by big, crazy parties.
- Always wait for people to ask before helping them out.
- Don't need to share news to make it real.
- Believe in yourself even if no one's giving you any feedback.
- Like periods of time with no plans.
- Like to kick it alone every now and then.
- Can't stand people who talk during the movie.

sensors vs. intuitives

This part of your personality is about how you take in information from the world around you. Do you like your facts hard or fuzzy? Do you need physical proof, or do you trust your gut? Do you have to see to believe, or can you believe what you can't see? Does your intuition mean more to you than logic?

In each row pick the word or phrase that best describes you. Keep track of how many you select from column a and how many you select from column b.

a

1. Motto: Just The Facts
2. Time is money
3. Life is in the details
4. All the small things
5. Literal
6. Sports is stats
7. Specific
8. Watch one show until it's over
9. Make a plan
10. Daydreaming is a waste of time
11. Multiple choice

b

Motto: Trust Your Gut
Time is relative
Life is the big picture
All the big ideas
Figurative
Sports is passion
General
Channel surf constantly
Wing it
Daydreaming is fun
Essay question

If you chose more from column a than column b, well, you're a Sensor. If you chose more from column b, you're an Intuitive.

if you're a *sensor,* guess you:

- Go for the hard facts instead of trusting your intuition.
- Always know what time it is and are always on time.
- Love details but sometimes get bogged down in them.
- Seem alert all the time.
- Stick with the facts—after all, anything that's not a fact isn't really the truth.
- Need proof—if you can prove it, it's real; otherwise, forget it.
- Pay attention to what's on your plate here and now.
- Know every detail of a movie's plot but struggle when asked about its vibe or mood.

if you're an *intuitive,* guess you:

- Like to use your intuition instead of hard facts (yeah, try *that* on a chemistry final!).
- Never know exactly what time it is.
- Don't deal well with details and sometimes ignore them.
- Get tagged as a space case every now and then.
- Look for the meaning behind the facts.
- Believe there's more to life than what exists in reality.
- Think about what's coming up next instead of focusing on what's here and now.
- Are more interested in the vibe or mood of a movie than its plot.

thinkers vs. feelers

This part is all about how you make decisions. It's kind of like part two (intuitives vs. sensors) in that it's about your gut versus your intellect, but instead of defining how you take in information, it's about what you do with it. Do you make choices carefully? Or do you use hunches instead?

In each row pick the word or phrase that best describes you. Keep track of how many you select from column a and how many you select from column b.

a

1. Decisive
2. Cool, calm, collected
3. Look out for number one
4. Love to argue—but not fight
5. Facts rule
6. Don't take things personally
7. Never take it back
8. Respect your own decisions
9. Always decide
10. Choose for yourself
11. Like having things clear always

b

Not so sure

Aw, freak out!

Wonder what everyone else needs

Don't like to argue or fight— and they're the same thing!

Intuition rules

Often take things personally

Often change your mind

Respect others' decisions

Sometimes avoid deciding

Try to make everyone happy

Don't mind a little gray area

If you chose more from column a than column b, you're a Thinker. If you chose more from column b, you're a Feeler. Here's the deal.

if you're a *thinker,* chances are you:

- Are great under pressure.
- Like to argue just for the hell of it . . . whether you care about the outcome or not.
- Know what you should take personally and what you shouldn't.
- Appreciate it when others are consistent.
- Stick to your guns, even if other people say you're wrong.
- Don't worry about decisions you've already made.
- Sometimes wonder if people think you're icy cold.
- Don't allow yourself to be taken advantage of.
- Gotta have things done right, even if some people aren't happy.
- Don't mind offending people if that's what you need to do.

if you're a *feeler,* chances are you:

- Can flake under pressure.
- Don't like to argue unless you need to—it's not your idea of fun.
- Take things personally—sometimes a little, sometimes a lot.
- Don't mind when others change their minds.
- Rethink your point of view if others disagree.
- Wonder if you did the right thing.
- Sometimes wonder if people just think you're a space cadet.
- Go out of your way to help others, even when it's a pain in the neck.
- Try to make sure everyone is as happy as possible, even if decisions don't get made.
- Hate pissing people off, and hate conflict.

perceivers vs. judgers

So, how do you like to run your life? Do you like things spontaneous and unpredictable? Or are you better when you're in charge all day long, no surprises? Or do you like a little bit of both?

In each row pick the word or phrase that best describes you. Keep track of how many you select from column a and how many you select from column b.

a

- 1. Sometimes late
- 2. Channel surf
- 3. Easily distracted
- 4. Spontaneous
- 5. Love surprises
- 6. Prefer "creative" answers
- 7. Be flexible!
- 8. Exciting
- 9. Procrastinate
- 10. New haircut every few months
- 11. Don't mind getting lost—sometimes adventures rule!

b

Always on time
Read *TV Guide*
Good attention span
Scheduled
Hate surprises
Prefer "correct" answers
Be prepared!
Dependable
Get it done
Same hair as last year—hey, it looks good; why change it?
Hate getting lost and never do

If you chose more from column a than column b, you're a Perceiver. If you chose more from column b, you're a Judger. Here's the deal.

if you're a *perceiver*, bet you:

- Don't have a PalmPilot (or wish you didn't).
- Have a messy bedroom.
- Change the subject a lot.
- Sometimes find your wallet empty.
- Don't always finish what you start.
- Can't deal with alarm clocks—you'll get up on time (you hope).
- Wait to see how you feel before deciding what to wear.
- Love to shop.
- Don't mind changing plans frequently.
- Borrow stuff from friends and sometimes forget that you did.

if you're a *judger*, bet you:

- Have a PalmPilot (or wish you did).
- Are usually pretty neat 'n' tidy.
- Hate it when people keep changing the subject.
- Rarely run out of cash.
- Always finish what you start.
- Set the alarm before hitting the sack, even on Friday nights.
- Think about your outfit the night before.
- Hate to shop, love to buy.
- Hate it when plans change . . . that's when things fall apart.
- Can't stand borrowing stuff and hate being in debt.

Okay, So Now What?

So you've learned a thing or two about yourself already. But there's more! First, remind yourself how you answered the four questions.

1. You're an Extrovert✓ or an Introvert
2. You're a Sensor ✓ or an Intuitive
3. You're a Thinker ✓ or a Feeler
4. You're a Perceiver✓ or a Judger

Put them all together, and what do you get?

Extrovert-Intuitive-Thinker-Judger?
Introvert-Sensor-Feeler-Perceiver?
Or what?

You'll see that when you combine your types, there's even more to it than you thought there would be. Here are the sixteen combinations, with a rundown on what each one's all about.

tucker says

I've taken this test, or a variation of it, about four thousand times. Half the time I come up Extroverted-Intuitive-Feeler-Perceiver, half the time I come up Introverted-Intuitive-Feeler-Perceiver. I think it has to do with the time of day. I'm a full introvert in the morning, but as the sun moves west, I get a little more extroverted. Guess I'm not a morning person. Either way, I'm definitely an Intuitive (always), a Feeler (most of the time), and a total Perceiver. Just so you know. :-)

introvert-intuitive-thinker-judger

Why you rule: You're optimistic, organized, hopeful, and committed.
Why you don't: You're critical.

About you: You see the world as one big opportunity for change and improvement. You honestly like to make things better for everyone. And even though everyone might not see it all the time, you always do more than your share. You're trustworthy and honest most of the time, and you tell the truth even when people might not want to hear it.

introvert-intuitive-feeler-judger

Why you rule: You're caring, wise, accepting, and inspiring.
Why you don't: You're distant.

About you: If anyone's on the down low, it's you. You'd much rather do something good for someone else and let it go at that than deal with the whole being-thanked-and-patted-on-the-back thing. You're incredibly respectful of other people's space, even if they haven't asked you to be. In fact, sometimes they wonder where the hell you are.

introvert-sensor-feeler-judger

Why you rule: You're easygoing, dependable, open-minded, and you have a neat bedroom.
Why you don't: You're easy to take advantage of.

About you: It's a good thing you're around—you're the ultimate cry-on-my-shoulder rock. You're admired for your unique ability to "be there" for a friend in a way no one else can. And you're undemanding. Unfortunately, some people take this for granted and walk all over you. Jerks.

introvert-sensor-thinker-judger

Why you rule: You're responsible, respectful, idealistic, and you're always on your best behavior.

Why you don't: You're impatient.

About you: No matter what situation you're in, you know exactly the right thing to do. No one's ever been able to blame you for acting inappropriately. You behave. And boy, do you ever get annoyed and impatient when others don't.

introvert-intuitive-thinker-perceiver

Why you rule: You're flexible, thoughtful, clever, and you can read any situation.

Why you don't: You're a space case.

About you: People are constantly surprised at what comes out of your mouth—you seem like you're not even paying attention much of the time, but you can sum up the important stuff in life in about three words or less. Of course, you may see things in a completely different way tomorrow, you may even contradict yourself, but hey, that's life, right?

introvert-intuitive-feeler-perceiver

Why you rule: You're easygoing, idealistic, complex, and strong.

Why you don't: You're hard to understand.

About you: You'd never tell anyone else what to do, but you're pretty harsh on yourself. It's this mix of easygoing and strict that confuses people . . . they often don't expect you to have as much strength—and stubbornness—as you do. They think they know you, then they don't.

introvert-sensor-feeler-perceiver

Why you rule: You're sensitive, calm, encouraging, and you bring people together.
Why you don't: You're lazy.

About you: Even if you don't consider yourself an artist, you can be sure art or music or some kind of creative expression plays a big role in your life. Thing is, you feel more comfortable expressing yourself that way than you do, like, talking to people. Does that mean you're deep or shy? Probably both.

introvert-sensor-thinker-perceiver

Why you rule: You're aware, ambitious, spontaneous, and you're up for almost anything.
Why you don't: You're aloof.

About you: You know that person who kind of hangs around the edges, not really saying anything, just checking things out, then all of a sudden says the funniest thing you've ever heard? Of course you do—it's you. So how come you don't hang around long enough for people to really get to know you?

extrovert-intuitive-thinker-perceiver

Why you rule: You're forward thinking, speedy, active, and inventive.
Why you don't: You don't have the best follow-through.

About you: You're an optimist, that's for sure—as far as you're concerned, you're gonna make it after all. If you believe, you can achieve. Dreams can come true! And all that other stuff. But don't forget, making it means working it. It's not all about dreaming—it's about doing, too.

extrovert-intuitive-feeler-perceiver

Why you rule: You're enthusiastic, magnetic, entertaining, and optimistic.

Why you don't: You're in my face.

About you: Look up *life of the party* in the dictionary, and there's probably a picture of you, raising the roof in a VIP room somewhere. You're a blast to have around because you're always excited about stuff. But sometimes you forget that life isn't a 24/7 house party . . . the beat needs a break every now and then. Chill.

extrovert-sensor-feeler-perceiver

Why you rule: You're positive, accepting, energetic, and present in the here and now.

Why you don't: You're self-absorbed.

About you: A day in the life of you is always interesting, memorable, and unpredictable. That's because —you'd never put up with boredom for more than a moment. You act—now. The problem is, sometimes you act before you think and find yourself pissing people off.

extrovert-sensor-thinker-perceiver

Why you rule: You're motivated, quick, busy, and you've got your finger on the pulse.

Why you don't: You're insensitive.

About you: You hate going to sleep—who knows what kind of party you might be missing? Besides, who needs rest? You've got plenty of energy! Oh, and forget planning your night —you'd rather just wing it and see where life takes you. But check yourself: Some people feel way more comfortable playing it safe, and it's not fair for you to dis them about it. Respect.

extrovert-sensor-thinker-judger

Why you rule: You're focused, smart, popular, and in charge.
Why you don't: You're pushy.

About you: It's all about taking advantage of every opportunity life presents you and rocking. No challenge is too great for you because you've got the energy, brains, and drive to win—sometimes at all costs. You're quick to ask others for a hand when you need it. Except sometimes you don't ask—you just tell people what to do. Don't you?

extrovert-intuitive-feeler-judger

Why you rule: You're perceptive, understanding, ingenious, and you're a great communicator.
Why you don't: You're manipulative.

About you: You seem to know exactly what everyone's thinking at any given time, and you're a terrific listener. You're amazing with words, and you're the world's expert on how to cheer people up. You truly have everyone's best interests at heart. The only thing is, they didn't know what their best interests were until you told them.

extrovert-sensor-feeler-judger

Why you rule: You're alert, caring, admired, and stylish.
Why you don't: You avoid dealing with stuff.

About you: Who's got it together? You do! Yep, you're on time, you look fantastic, and you've got admirers in every class. You've got your business tight. Who's to say you don't? Well, you. Because you know, better than anyone, that you blow off situations you're not up for. News flash—pleasant or not, you still have to deal.

extrovert-sensor-thinker-judger

Why you rule: You're outgoing, dependable, and funny, and you love people.

Why you don't: You're bossy.

About you: If you're not the class clown, you're probably funnier than she is . . . no one's better at the snappy comeback than you are. And even if you offend people, you have a gift for charming them back. You're dependable and great to have around. But what's with the control freakiness you perpetrate every now and then?

 Check page 157 for where to find out more about psychological profiling.

what brain wave are you on?

HERE'S SOMETHING THAT SUCKS: MOST OF THE
world tends to think that either you're smart or you're not so smart. I
guess it's easier to divide people up that way. But you know it's not
that simple. You know people who are great at math but hopeless in
music class. You know people who always understand what you're
thinking, but they can't write a term paper to save their lives. In other
words, not everyone's smart in the same way. In fact, not everyone's
stupid in the same way, either. Right?

For centuries people have been trying to define intelligence and
to determine who has it and who doesn't. What am I talking about
when I say "intelligence"? Good question. I should be more specific.
These days most people use the word to mean ways of learning and
using information. As in, how you take in information, make sense of
it, and decide what to do with it.

But during the late 1980s and early 1990s this doctor named
Howard Gardner came up with the idea that not only is everyone
intelligent, everyone is intelligent in *seven different* ways. We'll break
it down later, but here are the seven types of intelligence: Logical,
Verbal, Athletic, Spatial, Musical, Interpersonal, and Intrapersonal.

Now, he also said that some people are *more* intelligent than others in certain ways—like some people have lots of spatial intelligence and some have only a little—but make no mistake: We all have all seven types.

What's cool to figure out, though, is this: Which type is strongest in you? Which is weakest? What kind of balance do you have up there in your head?

Read each of the following profiles. Decide how well each one describes you, and rate it on a scale of 1 to 5 (5 meaning it fits you perfectly, 1 meaning nothing in it really sounds right). At the end of the chapter, pull together your ratings for an overall profile that will show you your strongest and weakest intelligence areas.

By the way, when you're assigning numbers to the seven profiles, keep this in mind: Choosing a 1 doesn't necessarily mean you're not smart when it comes to that area; it just means that in contrast to the other types, it's not your strongest. And choosing a 5 doesn't mean you're Einstein; it just means that in contrast to the others, it's one of your strongest. Remember, we all bring something different to the party.

The Brainiac

logical/mathematic intelligence

Algebra

about you:

Sure, everyone knows you don't have to struggle too hard in algebra, but the big secret is, you also kind of like it. Admit it, you get that special little tingle when you solve a really complex equation, don't ya? And you get that same little charge when you beat your kid sister at a game of checkers.

at school:

You're not just a whiz at math—you're also probably really good at science and history. Why? Because you love to put things in order; you love facts and data. Experimenting is your middle name—you're amazing at trying things out and making sense of them. Most people look at sports scores and see a bunch of numbers. You look at them and see a pattern, one that means something.

give it a shot:

Who wants to be a millionaire? You do, and you could be. Why should adults make all the money in the stock market? You've got a Web connection—use it to check out some of those on-line investing sites everyone seems to be striking it rich on. If anyone's gonna make a million before age 25, it's you. That is, if you get on it. So get on it!

your future:

Let's talk about science; let's talk about investment banking; let's talk about computer programming; let's even talk about raising money to make movies. See a pattern here? Because you're so good at making things fit together, you can make just about anything work.

the Word Smith
linguistic intelligence

about you:
When people talk about "book smart," they're probably talking about you. You seem to know every word in the dictionary (and when you don't know a word, you actually enjoy looking it up . . .), you shock people with your crossword-puzzle brilliance, and you remember every piece of trivia you've ever heard.

at school:
You're out of control when it comes to learning other languages, and your creative-writing assignments kick butt. Linguistic intelligence doesn't mean you'll have the most incredible ideas in English class, but it does mean that your teacher's gonna like your clever writing style. Bet you read a lot, but you look for more than a good plot or cool characters— you look for smart writing and sharp dialogue, too. You learn easily from books and lectures, and you probably pass your fair share of notes.

give it a shot:
Join the debate team, dude. You can talk anyone into a corner. While you're at it, start making plans for all the prize money you could win on the quiz shows. Oh, and try entering a poetry contest. You'll win.

your future:
You oughta be a rap star, the way you put words together. You can find a rhyme for anything, and it'll be a good one. Not feeling it? Consider these careers: TV writer. Teacher. Journalist. Advertising copywriter. Sportscaster. Novelist. Editor. Public relations person. Veejay.

the body
physical/athletic intelligence

about you:

If anyone's going to represent their country at the Olympics, it's going to be you. Not into any of the Olympic sports? You'll be scoring points (and hotties!) at the X-games or knocking them dead in ballet class. Yep, you're in tune with your body, and you often feel like your body is an extension of your brain. You *think* with your fingers. (Sound strange? Ask an athlete. They'll tell you.)

at school:

Sitting still for an entire period is a major accomplishment for you. Not because you're not interested in what's going on—you just wish you could hear about it outside, or while you're punching a boxing bag, or over a game of Ping-Pong. Sure, you understand what the biology teacher is saying about plasma and stuff, but wouldn't it be so much easier to understand if she could just put out a bucket of it for you to dunk your hands in and *feel?*

give it a shot:

Grab the stage on open-mike night and throw down a comedy routine. Not of the Seinfeld variety; more like Jim Carrey. Your talent at mimicking other people's movements and expressions is bound to get some laughs. (If it doesn't, you'll be spry enough to dodge incoming tomatoes.)

your future:

Actually, you're probably not reading this, because you're already out there training for the Olympics or trying to go pro. Not into sports? Think about being a dancer, landscaper, stunt double, zookeeper, construction worker, potter, carpenter, or anything else that involves using your body and hands every day.

The Gravity master

spatial intelligence

about you:

And the award for best cinematography goes to: you. Ditto for production design, costume design, and makeup. Oh, and you won't get lost on the way home from the awards ceremony—you have no problem finding your way around these parts—or any other parts, for that matter. Spatial intelligence is all about knowing how things fit together, how they work, and how to make them look cool. You know where you stand, literally, all the time and where everything else around you stands, too.

at school:

No one gets more out of a map or chart or graph than you do. Where everyone else sees lines and icons, you see a story, with meaning. As in, "Of course Kazakhstan and Iran have so many foods in common. They both border the Caspian Sea. See?" And while everyone else comes up with cute little ways to remember the placement of organs in that frog you're dissecting, you just seem to know where everything goes. Not to mention how you seem to know where everyone in the room is standing and in which direction they're moving all the time.

give it a shot:

Grab a camera or sketch pad (if you haven't already) and start keeping a visual record of your life. After all, diaries don't have to be written. Use the language you understand best.

Sure, we all want to be special-effects whizzes, but with your spatial intelligence and knack for making things look cool, you could actually do it. In fact, any kind of design, from fashion to interiors to print, to products like cars and computers, is right up your alley. You're a natural race car driver. Environmental careers could be your calling, especially ones that actually get you out there climbing a mountain or two. Oh, and you could be a star in the world of architecture.

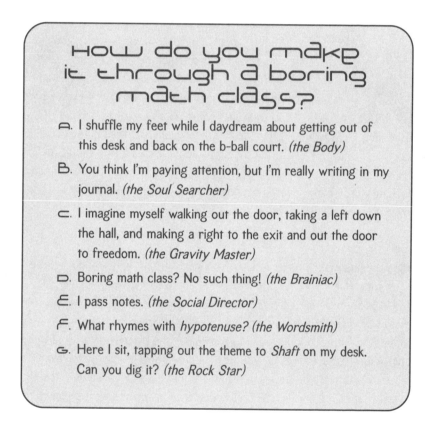

How do you make it through a boring math class?

A. I shuffle my feet while I daydream about getting out of this desk and back on the b-ball court. *(the Body)*

B. You think I'm paying attention, but I'm really writing in my journal. *(the Soul Searcher)*

C. I imagine myself walking out the door, taking a left down the hall, and making a right to the exit and out the door to freedom. *(the Gravity Master)*

D. Boring math class? No such thing! *(the Brainiac)*

E. I pass notes. *(the Social Director)*

F. What rhymes with *hypotenuse*? *(the Wordsmith)*

G. Here I sit, tapping out the theme to *Shaft* on my desk. Can you dig it? *(the Rock Star)*

The ROCK Star

musical intelligence

about you:
For you, silence sucks. A moment without a tune in it is incomplete. Can't hear me? Take your headphones off and listen up. Bet you're still tapping out a beat.

at school:
On the first day of school you made a beeline for the music department. That is, unless you realized that, like in almost every school in the country, your music program, well, bites. The fact is, of all seven types of intelligence, musical is the one that gets ignored the most. In fact, most musically brilliant people don't even know they have it in them because they were never encouraged to develop it. The good news is, musically brilliant people bring music into every part of their lives, with or without musical training. Tell *that* to your mother next time she makes you turn down your stereo while studying.

give it a shot:
Sure, you can play music . . . but can you *write* it? Start coming up with your own beats and melodies, and see where it takes you! Surely you can do better than most of what's in the Top 40.

your future:
Save the music! No, seriously, musically gifted people have a responsibility to keep the rest of the world dancing and singing. That could mean performing, or producing, or choreographing, or teaching, or anything where you get to have music playing all day. Oh, and you're in charge of the mix tape for the next party.

The Social Director

interpersonal intelligence

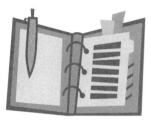

about you:

Pin a Social Director tag on your chest because you're a pro at entertaining the mob. Not that you're always out to make everyone's day better, but there's no doubt that you can win friends, influence people, and understand exactly what makes them tick almost instantly.

at school:

It takes you just one glance at a clique for you to know not only who's in charge but who *used to be* in charge, who's on the way out, who's on the way up, and who's dating who. And why. And you can use this information to smooth things over (or rile things up, depending on your mood). You do best in class-participation situations, especially mock trials or group reports. You're probably the first one picked for any team or committee—not only because you're good at it but because you know how to get people psyched.

give it a shot:

Yeah, you're a genius when it comes to your own peers, but do your talents transfer to other age groups? Find a way to spend some time with people older or younger than you are—maybe even some senior citizens or preschoolers—and challenge yourself to be a leader in those situations, too.

your future:

Get yourself a slogan—you'll be running for office. Why? Because you seem to understand what everyone needs, and you know how to get people to rally around you. Can't stomach politics? Get a talk show like everyone else. Or go for teaching, public relations, consulting, counseling, party planning—anything that lets you help people solve problems.

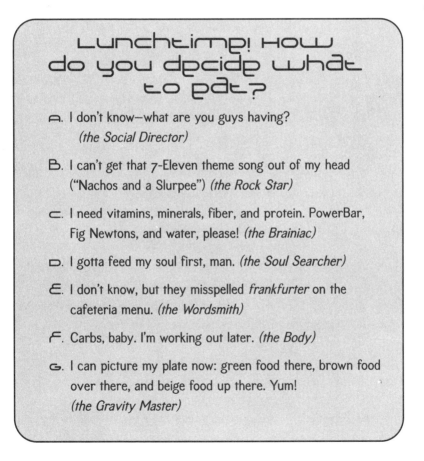

Lunchtime! How do you decide what to eat?

A. I don't know—what are you guys having?
   (the Social Director)

B. I can't get that 7-Eleven theme song out of my head ("Nachos and a Slurpee") *(the Rock Star)*

C. I need vitamins, minerals, fiber, and protein. PowerBar, Fig Newtons, and water, please! *(the Brainiac)*

D. I gotta feed my soul first, man. *(the Soul Searcher)*

E. I don't know, but they misspelled *frankfurter* on the cafeteria menu. *(the Wordsmith)*

F. Carbs, baby. I'm working out later. *(the Body)*

G. I can picture my plate now: green food there, brown food over there, and beige food up there. Yum!
   (the Gravity Master)

The Soul Searcher

intrapersonal intelligence

about you:

Hey, you! Yeah, you! I bet you're catching some flak for not hanging with the crew. Don't worry about them—they just don't understand that for you, happiness doesn't mean being surrounded by a posse 24/7. The truth is, you know yourself, and believe in yourself, way more than they ever will. And by the way, rad outfit!

at school:

Your two favorite words when it comes to school are *independent study*. If you had your way, you'd never sit through another history lecture—I mean, what's the point if you could be out there digging up pottery and bones for real? On the social front, you probably have plenty of friends. People are attracted to your individuality and self-confidence, but you're just as happy walking home solo. And don't freak about that lousy grade you got in English—that stupid teacher just didn't understand the brilliance of your totally out-there essay.

give it a shot:

You know, sports isn't all about teams. Board sports, track, cross-country, singles tennis, biking, and skating all take you deeper inside yourself, challenging you to use what you already know and to learn more. Besides, when it comes to winning on race day, being able to deal mentally is just as important as being able to deal physically.

your future:
There's nothing you couldn't do if you wanted to . . . but whatever you do, you better care deeply about it. You have very little time to deal with things that don't really speak to you. And no one's better at working alone: so think about scientific research, archaeology, and even teaching. Especially independent study. :-)

Now that you've read each description and given yourself a ranking, you've got your profile. It should kinda look like mine, (see below) but with your own ratings, of course

tucker says

Here's how I'd rank myself

Logical—3

Verbal—4

Athletic—4

Spatial—2

Musical—2

Interpersonal—5

Intrapersonal—1

So what's that make me? I guess it makes me a crowd manipulator with good verbal skills to get my message across and good athletic skills to make a get-away when the crowd gets annoyed with me!

Check page 157 for where to find out more on the seven types of intelligence.

your

palms

what's in the
palm of your hand?

WHAT CAN THE SHAPE OF YOUR HAND AND THE
lines of your palm tell you? Well, for thousands of years, since the
early days of Egypt and India, palmistry experts have believed that
a long, hard look at your hands can tell who you are and where
you're going in life. No one has a hand shape, or pattern of palm
lines and bumps, quite like yours—your hands tell a story that's as
unique as you are.

Read about the different hand shapes and pick the hand that
looks most like yours (you obviously won't find an exact match,
but come as close as you can . . .). What's its story?

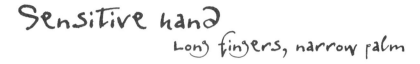

Sensitive hand
Long fingers, narrow palm

Your hands are like little extensions of your brain—to truly understand something, you need to touch it. The world is full of magic for you, and you love soaking it all in. You're constantly learning and growing from new experiences, and while change causes most people to freak out, it doesn't bother you at all. In fact, you embrace it, often making changes in yourself along the way (that's why people never know what you're going to look like: surf rat one minute, rock star the next, total prep the next). But even as you shape shift through life, you have a knack for reminding people (usually by touching them with your sensitive hands) that you're still you.

Passionate hand
Short fingers, narrow palm

You're emotional, you're creative, and you love to feel the highs, and the lows, of that crazy roller coaster we call life. (Cue country music sound track here. . . .) Some people see your attitude as moody; you just see it as being *alive*. No one shows the love more than you (to anyone who's worthy)—but no one has a hotter temper, either. Bet your ex is still stinging from that harsh breakup y'all had. But hey, you had to follow your heart and take a different path . . . after all, your intuition is stronger than anyone else's, and you've learned to rely on it.

Practical hand
Short fingers, wide palm

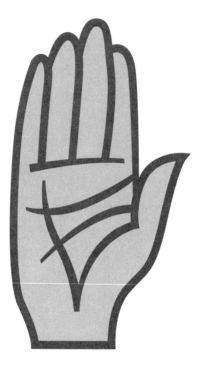

You're reliable, strong, and dependable, and you work hard. You're probably interested in nature, and you know you love getting dirt on your hands and sand in your sneakers. People look to you for common-sense advice because they know they can count on you to be grounded. You care a lot about keeping the peace, you follow the rules, and even on those days when you give some serious thought to rocking a sleeve-less concert tee and leather cuffs, you tend to stick to your habits.

intellectual hand
Long fingers, wide palm

Hey, you with the brain! Your hands say you've got logic and reason to spare—and you're such a good communicator that you're able to explain it all to the rest of us. Your quick mind, along with your confidence, independence, and optimism, make you a born leader—so say hello to the student council presidency. Or team captainship. Or any other role where you can inspire others. Sure, some people may claim you're a little out of touch with your emotions, but you probably think they're all a bunch of flakes, anyway.

tucker says
I've got an intellectual hand shape. Which may or may not come as a surprise to people who know me.

Line it Up

Your palm has literally dozens of lines, bumps, folds, and dimples, all of which mean something very specific and unique to a serious palm expert. In order to truly understand the ins and outs of palmistry, you'd need to study it for years and years.

So, rather than trying to get all complicated, let's just take a quick look at the major lines on your palm. Keep in mind that the size, depth, or length of certain lines don't necessarily indicate the most obvious outcomes. In other words, don't panic if you have a short life line. It doesn't mean you'll have a short life. And if you can't see all of your lines that clearly, try cupping your hands a tiny bit.

heart line

head line

fate line

life line

The Heart Line

This line begins underneath your pinkie and runs across the top of your palm. The heart line is all about your feelings, emotions, and, yes, romance. A deeper or longer line might indicate that love and romance are more important to you than most things in your life, but it doesn't mean that you're more likely to have good relationships. Shorter or fainter love lines might mean you're more independent than romantic, but that doesn't necessarily mean you won't have superlong love affairs.

The Head Line

This is the line that runs below and parallel to the heart line. The head line doesn't show whether you're smart or not—it shows how you think. The longer, deeper, and straighter the line, the more likely you are to use clear reason and logic when making choices. The shorter, fainter, and more broken up the line, the more likely you are to use intuition and other creative ways of processing information and making decisions.

The Life Line

The life line kind of winds around your thumb area, enclosing the thumb and that fleshy part it springs from. The life line doesn't indicate how long you'll live or anything like that. What it does measure is how active and energetic you are. A deep, long, well-defined life line means you're the kind of person who wakes up every morning wanting to add to your list of things to do. A shorter, fainter, or more broken life line might mean you prefer a quieter, slower pace.

The Fate Line

Your fate line runs vertically through the middle of your palm, from the base of your palm up to the head line or heart line. It indicates how comfortable you'll be living the life you choose. As in, those people who really seem like they know what they're doing all the time, probably have vivid fate lines. The rest of us, the ones who aren't ever quite sure whether they're where they're supposed to be, have fainter ones.

tucker says

My heart line is deep but short (meaning love's important to me but not that important), my head line is shallow and wavy (meaning I use intuition more than logic), my life line is shallow (meaning I'm mellow) and my fate line is deep, but broken (meaning I don't always know what I'm doing).

Check page 157 for where to find out more on palm reading.

your sun sign

what's your
sign in western astrology?

OKAY, SO YOU READ YOUR HOROSCOPE EVERY
morning. You hope it has a clue in there about what's in store for
you, who you might meet, or where the day might take you. But
astrology is good for way more than predicting the future. Your
sign says a lot about who you are in the here and now, how you
deal with other people, and what you think of yourself.

When people talk about your *sign*, they're usually talking about
your sun sign. But Western astrology is about a lot more than
that—your moon sign, your rising signs, houses, planets, and all
kinds of other stuff also plays a big role. I could go into a long spiel
about how it all works (it's based on movements of planets and
stars) and where it comes from (no one really knows) and why we
start the zodiac in March instead of January (because the astrological year begins with the first day of spring) and everything like
that, but who needs it? (If *you* do . . . just check out the list of books
to read at the back of this book. . . .) I'm just gonna cut right to the
good stuff.

If you don't know what your sun sign is, check this table:

if you were born between: your sun sign is:

MARCH 22—APRIL 20   Aries

APRIL 21—MAY 21   Taurus

MAY 22—JUNE 22   Gemini

JUNE 23—JULY 23   Cancer

JULY 24-AUGUST 23   Leo

AUGUST 24—SEPTEMBER 23   Virgo

If you're born right at the edge of two signs, consider yourself a "cusp baby"—and always pay attention to both signs. My mother's that way, right on the edge of Leo and Virgo. (Hi, Ma.)

SEPTEMBER 24—OCTOBER 23 Libra

OCTOBER 24—NOVEMBER 22 Scorpio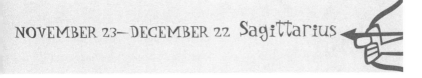

NOVEMBER 23—DECEMBER 22 Sagittarius

DECEMBER 23—JANUARY 19 Capricorn

JANUARY 20—FEBRUARY 19 Aquarius

FEBRUARY 20—MARCH 21 Pisces

Aries

dates: March 22-April 20
symbol: The Ram
quality: Cardinal (see page 148)
element: Fire (see page 151)

You rule because: You're brave, impulsive, and original.
But sometimes: You can be impatient.

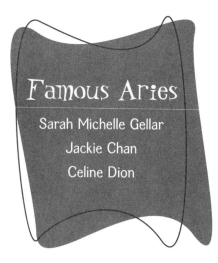

Famous Aries

Sarah Michelle Gellar
Jackie Chan
Celine Dion

the upside of Aries:

Ever seen *Road Rules*? What, you were on it? What a shock . . . not. You're just wild and crazy—and cool—enough to get on the show. Not only would the challenges be a breeze for you, but thanks to your enthusiasm and the, uh, sheer volume of your voice, the camera would be all up in your face the whole time. And admit it—you'd love it.

It's not just about being a risk taker. For you, it's about being a pioneer. See, the sun enters your sign right on the first day of spring—so you represent newness, growth, optimism, and energy. That means you're the first to try something new and the first to go somewhere different. You're also ambitious, and you truly believe that you *can* hit the goals you set for yourself—from burping the alphabet to getting into your first-choice college. You go for it, and you know going fot it is half the battle.

the downside of Aries:

You just gotta do *everything* yourself, don't you? You're all, "I can do it, and I'll do it my way!" Sorry, Aries . . . that may work in inspirational TV movies, but face it: You've gotta be willing and able to compromise and cooperate in this world. No lie: You *can't* hit the biggest goals in life without a little help and support. Oh, and a little patience.

your fashion sensibility:

Trendy. Fashion magazines are too slow for you—by the time they show something, you're over it. So . . . does that make you cutting edge or fashion victim? Just kidding. :-)

hidden talent:
Board games

Taurus

dates: April 21-May 21
symbol: The Bull
quality: Fixed (see page 149)
element: Earth (see page 150)

You rule because: You're dependable, loving, and productive.
But sometimes: You're a buzz kill.

the upside of Taurus:

You're strong; you're stable; you're steady. People know they can
count on you—you're always where you say you're gonna be, and
you're right on time, too. You always have a plan, and it's always a
good one. And no matter what's going on around you, you manage to
be cool, calm, collected. Oh, and thanks for not
being all moody. You're one of those
people who, if you're smiling, there's
not some weird thing going on
underneath—you're just happy. And
you're not gonna go ballistic at the
drop of a hat.

You're kind and generous,
Taurus, and your friends,
who you always keep
for life, mean the
world to you.
There's no way
you'd leave a friend
alone on prom night,
and there's no way
you'd vote against

them in the school election—even if you thought the other candidate was better.

the downside of Taurus:

No way anyone, or anything, is gonna get in your way. Besides, you've already made a plan, so why should you change it? Here's the thing, Taurus— sometimes the best things in life happen *without* a plan. In fact, sometimes the best things in life happen when the plan totally falls apart. Go ahead, let yourself get distracted every now and then.

Famous Tauruses

Kirsten Dunst
Busta Rymes
Lance Bass

your fashion sensibility:

Durable. When you go shopping, you're thinking about what you're going to use those clothes for, not just how they're going to look. After all, what matters more?

hidden talent:

Singing

Gemini

dates: May 22-June 22
symbol: The Twins
quality: Mutable (see page 149)
element: Air (see page 152)

You rule because: You're curious, open-minded, and adventurous.
But sometimes: You're confusing.

the upside of Gemini:

People say that like a set of twins, you, Gemini, have two sides to your personality. They're wrong. You have about a zillion sides to your personality. And you use them all, all the time. All these sides of you mean you're versatile, adaptable, and ready for anything. No matter what opportunities show up during the course of a day, you'll be all over them. Not to suggest that you sit around waiting for opportunities—

Famous Geminis

Lenny Kravitz
Alanis Morissette
Josh Jackson

actually, you're all over the place, drumming them up, for yourself and for other people.

One thing all of your sides share is a seriously funny sense of humor. You love to laugh, and you love making other people laugh, too. Jokes, to you, are like vitamins—you need a certain recommended daily amount or you feel deprived. People love how you're always looking for new reasons to crack up. Oh, and you use language like no one else, so one-liners come easy.

the downside of Gemini:

Have a little trouble concentrating sometimes, Gemini? Not that you're the ADD poster child or anything, but you do tend to go from one thing to the next quickly. That means you get to experience a lot, sure, but . . . wait, keep reading, pay attention . . . sometimes life requires you to stay focused.

your fashion sensibility:

Ever changing. You like to see how you feel in the morning before picking out what you're going to wear. Your clothes reflect your mood.

hidden talent:

Trivia

Cancer

dates: June 23-July 23
symbol: The Crab
quality: Cardinal (see page 148)
element: Water (see page 151)

You rule because: You're sensitive, nurturing, and traditional.
But sometimes: You're moody.

the upside of Cancer:

Without you, Cancer, there'd never be any peace and quiet in this world. You're the one the rest of us turn to when things get crazy or hectic or scary or sad—you've got the gift of making everyone feel comfortable, protected, and confident. You're sentimental, and you love to hang out and look at old pictures, watch favorite movies, or make favorite meals—always with good, old friends.

You're emotional, but in an admirable way—you're not just a crier or complainer; you're a laugher and high fiver, too. You *feel* things. To keep perspective, you probably have a room or some other space that's a special sanctuary for you, and you spend a lot of time fixing it up so it's just the way you like

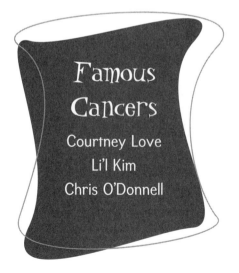

Famous Cancers

Courtney Love
Li'l Kim
Chris O'Donnell

it—with all your collections on full display. Oh, and I bet it's got a lot of CDs lying around it—you really *do* love your music.

the downside of Cancer:

Touchy, touchy! Oh, you're probably already mad at me for saying that. Sorry. But you are! See, you're sensitive. You feel life very intensely and all, but that means sometimes that you tend to take things way, way too seriously and personally. Sometimes those seemingly mean jokes from friends are really just jokes, and you should learn to laugh it off. That is, unless you *like* feeling dissed.

your fashion sensibility:

Comfortable. You like to look good, Cancer, but you know that the most important part of looking good is feeling comfortable. Guess that's why you look so hot in those sweats.

hidden talent:

Collecting (things that *mean* something to you)

Leo

dates: July 24-August 23
symbol: The Lion
quality: Fixed (see page 149)
element: Fire (see page 151)

You rule because: You're confident, creative, and helpful.
But sometimes: You're bossy.

the upside of Leo:

You're warm, you're generous, and you'll go way out of your way to make sure everyone's happy all the time. Helping people out comes as second nature to you—you love nothing more than to solve problems, especially when it makes things better for everyone. You're affection-ate, you're charming, you hug everyone in your path, and you're always up for a good time. Yo, Lion, they don't call you king of the jungle for nothing. You rule. See, because of your inclusive, helpful nature, people look to you when they need a leader. Good thing, too . . . because you're a natural at it. You want the best for everyone,

and you're willing to do what needs to be done and say what needs to be said to make it happen. You love making important decisions, you aren't afraid to tackle challenges, and you'll make sure everyone feels like a part of the team.

the downside of Leo:

How do I say this without ticking you off, Leo? Hmmm. You're a little bossy sometimes. But you knew that already, didn't you? Lose the attitude, Leo. See, we know you care about us, and we know you want us to be happy, but hey! We're people! Individuals! We like to do our own thing sometimes! Get the hint?

your fashion sensibility:

Designer only. That's right, Leo. The thought of spending way more money than you have on a new pair of jeans is a no-brainer for you. Of course you're gonna get the jeans!

hidden talent:
Party planning

Famous Leos

Bill Clinton
Whitney Houston
Madonna

Virgo

dates: August 24-September 23
symbol: The Virgin
quality: Mutable (see page 149)
element: Earth (see page 150)

You rule because: You're competent, logical, and in touch.
But sometimes: You're obsessive.

the upside of Virgo:

You're intelligent. You're organized. You're hardworking. You're articulate. You're capable. You're efficient. You live a healthy life. All that, and you're modest, too. In other words, you rock. See, you've got an extra dose of energy to get things done when the rest of us are exhausted. And that same something lets you make sense out of stuff that confuses the hell out of the rest of us. And not only does that put you at least a step or two in front of everyone else, it makes the world a better place in the meantime.

You know who's who, who's doing who, who's fighting with who, and who's wearing who. Not that you're a freak with gossip or anything, but your brain is so sharp and you pay such good attention that everyone's details just kind of soak into your head and stay there. And isn't it funny how the more you know, the more people tell you,

Famous Virgos

Moby
Cameron Diaz
Keanu Reeves

too? Good thing you have that internal filing system that helps you make sense of all of it.

the downside of Virgo:

It's not easy to be you, Virgo. You see problems other people totally ignore, and they bother you. Unfortunately, you feel that everyone else should be bothered, too, even when they don't see the problems. It's called perfectionism, and it's a losing battle, Virgo. Admit it: You'll do everything in the universe to get things up to your specifications, then go and raise your specifications. Won't you? It's enough to make you, and the rest of us, nuts. Take it easy!

your fashion sensibility:

Matching. You won't leave the house unless you're sure that what you're wearing constitutes a complete "outfit." Now, that's what I call discipline!

hidden talent:

Mind-body activities like yoga, martial arts, and meditation

Libra

dates: September 23-October 24
symbol: The Scales
quality: Cardinal (see page 148)
element: Air (see page 152)

You rule because: You're charming, fair, and peace loving.
But sometimes: You don't stick up for yourself.

The upside of Libra:

You're determined, Libra. Determined to have a life filled with harmony and balance. It's something you strive to bring into every moment, and we're all better off for it. You value nothing more than peace, fairness, and justice. You don't mind meeting anyone halfway, you always see both sides of a situation, and you're able to empathize with everyone involved, even if they aren't on your side.

You're smart as hell, and you love nothing more than to debate an issue—from both sides—just for the heck of it. (That is, as long as no one's feelings get hurt.) Oh, and you're also a big, huge romantic. Flowers, Valentine's Day, the works. But your date better have more to offer than tongue kisses and slow jams because you're a romantic from head to toe, not just you-know-where.

the downside of Libra:

Because you place so much importance on peace and harmony, sometimes you blow off your true feelings, or even blow off the truth, just to keep from pissing someone else off. And as a result, decisions get made that you don't like, or worse, they don't get made at all. Think that sucks? Flash forward to you, after the fact, stewing about how it all sucks. Now, is that peace? Not even. Learn to speak up, Libra. People *do* want to listen.

your fashion sensibility:
Simple

hidden talent:
Shopping

Famous Libras

Wyclef Jean
Janeane Garofalo
Mark McGwire

Scorpio

dates: October 24-November 22
symbol: The Scorpion
quality: Fixed (see page 149)
element: Water (see page 151)

You rule because: You're honest, goal oriented, and intense.
But sometimes: You're too competitive.

The upside of Scorpio:

If anyone's gonna sniff out the real deal in a situation, it's a Scorpio. Sure, you're interested in what's going on, but you're way more interested in *why* it's going on. You'll dig till you're satisfied, no matter what tough questions you have to ask and who you have to challenge in the process. And that's a good thing for the rest of us . . . otherwise we'd just bounce along, ignoring the tough stuff, even though we know it's important. Oh, and no one better tell you, "Don't go there." Because that's exactly where you will go.

When you set your sights on a goal, you'll do whatever it takes to make it there. People admire you for your guts and your staying power—even after the game is over, you're still playing. You've got sharp common sense, total focus, and amazing intuition. And you are mad, mad sexy. You make us swoon.

the downside of Scorpio:

Take it easy, Scorpio. You won, okay? I mean, of course you did. You started practicing before the rest of us even knew what the competition was about. In fact, we didn't even know it was a competition until you started informing us that we were losers. Listen, Scorpio—we like you just as much when you're not waving the trophy around in our faces. In fact, we like you more. So quit gloating. (Oh, and learn how to lose, too. You're the worst loser ever.)

Famous Scorpios

Winona Ryder
Bjork
Puff Daddy

your fashion sensibility:

Dress to impress. Impress that hottie you're trying to get with, that is. Yep, when you get dressed in the morning, you have one thing on your mind: sex appeal.

hidden talent:

Acting

Sagittarius

dates: November 23–December 22
symbol: The Archer
quality: Mutable (see page 149)
element: Fire (see page 151)

You rule because: You're optimistic, honest, and clever.
But sometimes: You're distant.

the upside of Sagittarius:

It's good to be a Sagittarius. Things don't get to you in quite the way they seem to get to other people. You're a fire sign, like Aries and Leo, which means you're energetic and enthusiastic, but you're a little more chill than they are. You're up for anything, but you're just as happy doing it at a lower volume. People don't get much past you, even though you sometimes let them think they do because life's more fun that way.

A Sagittarius who gets lost won't be lost for long—you're quick enough to figure out how to get home, and even if you can't, you'll probably make friends with whoever's around, so you'll at least feel at home. You can handle most situations, and you don't spend much time feeling doom and gloom . . . those are two things you can't deal with.

Famous
Sagittarians

Lucy Liu
Ben Stiller
Monica Seles

the downside of Sagittarius:

You have the-grass-is-always-greener disease. As in, you're always looking to the future or thinking about how good it would be *if* . . . , or daydreaming, or wishing you were somewhere or someone else. You're not always, uh, engaged in the moment. Which people think is all mysterious until they just start seeing it as annoying. You've got to struggle to pay attention—and you should because there's a lot going on in the here and now that you might enjoy. Oh, and you're always spending more cash than you should. That's gotta stop.

tucker says

Yep, I'm a Sagittarius. And the strange thing is, I really am. I mean, a lot of people are only kind of like what their sun sign says they should be, but I'm a die-hard Sag. What can I say?

your fashion sensibility:

Easily swayed. As soon as someone tells you that you look good in something, you're wearing it every day. And when they tell you it's tired, it's off you.

hidden talent:
Cooking

141

Capricorn

dates: December 23–January 19
symbol: The Goat
quality: Cardinal (see page 148)
element: Earth (see page 150)

You rule because: You're responsible, aware, and busy.
But sometimes: You're pessimistic.

the upside of Capricorn:

If you want something done, ask a Capricorn. (Note: Ask them nicely. Capricorns don't take orders well. Right?) See, you Caps tend to have a plan for the day, every day, and you won't hit the sack until you've knocked off each and every item on your to-do list. You know that unless you do it, it won't get done . . . while everyone else is just hoping things will happen as they sit around watching TV. You inspire the rest of us to try to be more organized.

You're really good with money—you don't spend what you don't have, and that means you'll end up rich one day. You're careful to plan for any changes, and you believe that nothing is impossible so long as you're prepared and willing to work superhard. You choose tough goals, and even when you can't see the light at the end of the tunnel, you're determined to work hard and persevere until you get there. Luckily you've got this wicked, unexpected sense of humor that keeps you rolling.

the downside of Capricorn:

Believe it or not, Capricorn, sometimes things *do* work out for the best whether you've made it happen or not. It's called luck, and it exists. In fact, some of us count on it. You, however, believe nothing good happens without working your butt off. Cut the pessimism, Capricorn—sometimes the world is in your corner just because.

your fashion sensibility:

Unchanging. You've been wearing a variation on the same outfit (could it be T-shirt and jeans?) for as long as you can remember. Well, as long as it works for you.

hidden talent:
Comedy

Famous Capricorns

Kid Rock
Mary J. Blige
Jared Leto

Aquarius

dates: January 20–February 19
symbol: The Water Bearer
quallty: Fixed (see page 149)
element: Air (see page 152)

You rule because: You're unique, independent, and ahead of your time.
But sometimes: You're flaky.

the upside of Aquarius:

Talk about ahead of your time. It's always a safe bet that whatever you're doing, wearing, or watching today—no matter how wack—is exactly what the rest of us will be doing, wearing, and watching tomorrow. You're charming, and even when people can't quite relate, they still think you're cute. You count fellow Aquarians as among your most important friends—it's like you guys have some sort of secret society or something.

You're ingenious. You can solve any problem. Maybe not exactly the same way everyone else would, but your solution will definitely be unique—and probably kind of fun. See, no matter what drudgery you have to deal with, from mowing the lawn to studying for trig, you'll find a way

Famous Aquarians

Justin Timberlake
Michael Jordan
Sarah McLachlan

to make it feel like a game. Oh, and you've got some seriously one-of-a-kind outfits . . . each one is flyer than the last.

the downside of Aquarius:

Uh, there's a world going on here, Aquarius, and if you want to be a part of it (and I know you do), you've gotta try a little harder to relate. Sure, you're way ahead of us most of the time, and even though that can be inspiring, sometimes it's just frustrating and annoying. You gotta try a little harder to clue in to us, to show up on time, and to remember the things that matter to other people. You care, so show it.

your fashion sense:

Zany. At least, that's what everyone else thinks. Really, you're just way ahead of your time. Keep it up.

hidden talent:

Technology whiz

Pisces

dates: February 20-March 21
symbol: The Fish
quality: Mutable (see page 149)
element: Water (see page 151)

You rule because: You're intuitive, imaginative, and wise.
But sometimes: You're vague.

the upside of Pisces:

Why limit yourself to five, or even six, senses? You're a Pisces, which means you have senses the rest of the world can't even conceive of, let alone understand. You get things on levels we don't even know exist, and the more practice you have using your intuition, the more perfect it becomes. Words are very important to you, but you also know there's usually way more going on than what's being said or discussed.

Word is that since you're the last sign in the zodiac, you actually combine all the traits of the other signs—you share all their characteristics, only you transform them into something different and truly amazing. You're much more interested in the essence of things and people than you are in hard facts or logic. You know the world's more complex than that. And the best part is, while your knowledge might seriously freak out people born under other signs, it doesn't bug you at all. You're optimistic about how complex things are, and that makes all of us a little more comfortable.

Famous Pisces

Drew Barrymore

Mia Hamm

Chelsea Clinton

the downside of Pisces:

Yeah, yeah, yeah. You're mysterious and mystical. You're an enigma. You're wiser than we are. But believe it or not, just because something seems basic or mundane to you doesn't mean it's not important to the rest of us. Take a minute to check in with the world—you might actually like it.

your fashion sensibility:

Light, airy, comfortable

hidden talent:

Water sports

Check page 157 for where to find out more about sun signs.

what quality
is your sign?

Every sun sign falls under one of three quality types: cardinal, fixed, or mutable. These three terms describe how people use their energy and how they focus their motivations.

Use this chart to figure out which quality your sign falls under.

if you are:	then your sign is:
Aries, Cancer, Libra, or Capricorn	Cardinal
Taurus, Leo, Scorpio, or Aquarius	Fixed
Gemini, Virgo, Sagittarius, Pisces	Mutable

cardinal

signs: Aries, Cancer, Libra, and Capricorn
key word: *Action!*
nickname: The starter

Cardinal signs like to start things. They use their energy to come up with new ideas, break new ground, open new doors . . . and to keep from getting bored. A day isn't complete for them unless something gets done—preferably something new and different. Cardinal signs like to test their limits. Any time of day you'll find them rearranging the living room, getting a new haircut, coming up with an extra-credit idea, or painting a mural on the garage door. They're busy, and they like it that way.

fixed

signs: Taurus, Leo, Scorpio, and Aquarius
key word: *Control*
nickname: The owner

Fixed signs like to wake up in the morning and know where everyone and everything is. Surprises aren't at the top of their list of favorite things—Fixed signs like to control their universe. People under Fixed signs have a good sense of what they're capable of, and they like to stick with what they know—don't ask them to push things (especially themselves) when slow and steady status quo is all they're really after. Sometimes Fixed signs like a plan, and sometimes they like to go on a whim, but they always like to be in control—it's their plan, or their whim, that they follow.

mutable

signs: Gemini, Virgo, Sagittarius, and Pisces
key word: *Adaptable*
nickname: The surfer

Mutable signs don't do well in situations where order and rules are what's important. They thrive on change—when the world is turning upside down, they don't freak and try to turn it back; they just look for ways to enjoy the ride. Mutable signs can face any kind of change, from having a substitute teacher to moving across the country, and make the best of it. Hell, they can even make it fun. Trying to control or change the world is a waste of energy, as far as they're concerned. Life is just a big old wave to be ridden.

what's your element?

Each of the twelve signs of the zodiac is connected to one of the four elements: Earth, Water, Fire, and Air. Throughout history these four have been considered the most basic building blocks of our planet—and each of us is especially influenced by one of them. Which element does your sign fall under?

earth

Taurus (April 21-May 21)
Virgo (August 24-September 23)
Capricorn (December 23-January 19)

Key word: *Physical*

People born under Earth signs are all about sensing, touching, seeing, hearing, smelling, and tasting the world around them. They're the kind of people who need to see and feel for them-selves. They gotta taste the pasta to know when it's done. They're the first to react to noises that are too loud and the first to pinch their noses when driving by the town dump. Earth people often touch friends when they're talking . . . and they love to give hugs. The downside? Earth people rarely trust their own intuition, let alone anyone else's. They're too focused on the physical.

water

Cancer (June 23-July 23)
Scorpio (October 24-November 22)
Pisces (February 20-March 21)

Key word: *Emotional*

Water sign people are driven by emotions. They're sympathetic, and they're a great ear when you're down. They care very deeply about other people's emotions, and when they say, "How ya doing?" they really mean it. Water babies are the least likely to "blame" someone when something goes wrong—instead they wonder how everyone will feel about the situation. Personal relationships are incredibly important to Water signs.

fire

Aries (March 22-April 20)
Leo (July 24-August 23)
Sagittarius (November 23-December 22)

Key word: *Instinctual*

Fire sign people run their lives based on instinct, trusting that life will be exciting and that intuition will guide them the

whole way through. Fire signs are the most psychic, and while they're interested in facts and other people's points of view, no outside force is going to make their decisions for them. They're all about listening to their guts. A Fire baby often seems removed or distant— because their connection to the inner self is much stronger than their connection to the real world and the people in it.

tucker says

I'm a Fire, in case you were wondering. Ouch! Stand back or you're gonna get burned, baby! And yep, I gotta say it fits. My intuition has always been stronger than my intellectual or my emotional self.

air

Gemini (May 22-June 22)
Libra (September 24-October 23)
Aquarius (January 20-February 19)

Key word: *Rational*

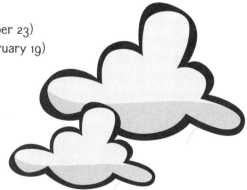

Thinking and reason are very important to Air signs. For something to ring true for them, it has to be logical. Air signs are classic communicators, and no one is better at bringing people together and putting ideas into words that everyone can understand. Things that don't make perfect sense don't mean much to Air signs—which is why you won't find too many of them composing experimental music or chasing UFOs. Air babies would much rather play a song that everyone can sing along to or throw a UFO-themed party for everyone they know.

Don't just read up on your own element—read everyone's. Why? Because there are always exceptions to every rule. Even though you're a Libra, you might really feel more like a Water than an Air.

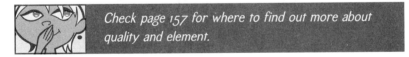

Check page 157 for where to find out more about quality and element.

outro

CONFUSED YET?

If you used this book right, you're probably a little confused. By now you've got over a dozen different analyses of who you are and why you are that way. Or at least a dozen different ways of looking at yourself. That is, if you read the whole thing.

But like I said up front, this book isn't about pinning you down or sticking a single label on you. It's about opening up your mind to who you are, who you aren't, who you might be, and who you want to be.

I hope it also gives you some clues about the other people in your life. I know for me, it helps a lot when I recognize certain things about other people. I'm able to adjust myself, and my attitude, accordingly. But beware: People, including you, change. And the minute you think you've got someone pinned down, they'll pull a switch on ya. Guaranteed.

So anyway, what are you supposed to do with all the results you picked up along the way? Well, lay them out. Think about what each one means. Then look for patterns. I bet you'll be surprised at how much of the stuff really matches up.

I mean, check out my results: I'm a 5, and right now I'm living in the third chakra. I'm a mesomorph Monkey with both right brain and left brain tendencies. I'm in the Thunderbird clan, I'm an Observer, and my Artemis side runs wild. I'm an Extrovert-Intuitive-Feeler-Perceiver (but sometimes I'm an Introvert). I'm strongest with Interpersonal intelligence, and I have an Intellectual palm. Oh, and I'm a Mutable Fire sign: Sagittarius.

That's a lot. But check this: All of my results say I'm optimistic. Adaptable. Energetic. Clever (but not necessarily book smart). Funny. Frequently disorganized. A little flaky. Distant. Too quick to spend money. Good with people. In love with the outdoors. And I agree with all this. Sure, a couple of things don't ring true. Like how supposedly I shouldn't really get along with Cancers, but in fact I love them. But I never would have given that any thought unless someone had told me otherwise—even though it wasn't on target, it did give me something to chew on. See what I mean?

So I hope you had fun. And I hope you do this: Keep tabs on your personality. Pay attention to how your results change over time. The way I see it, the more you know about yourself, the better you're able to deal. And rule.

later, tucker

for further reading

Want More?

Face it, you had so much fun with this book that you want more. Read these books. (I did! And they inspired me, big time.)

body type
Godwin, Malcolm. *Who Are You? 101 Ways of Seeing Yourself.* New York: Viking Penguin, 1999.

chakras
Pond, David. *Chakras for Beginners.* St. Paul, Minn.: Llewellyn Publications, 1999.

chinese astrology
Lau, Kenneth, and Theodore Lau. *The Handbook of Chinese Horoscopes.* New York: HarperCollins, 1999.

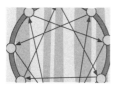

enneagram
Daniels, David, and V. Price. *The Essential Enneagram.* San Francisco: HarperCollins, 2000.

goddess wheel
Woolger, Jennifer Barker, and Roger Woolger. *The Goddess Within.* New York: Fawcett, 1989.

left brain/right brain
Godwin, Malcolm. *Who Are You? 101 Ways of Seeing Yourself.* New York: Viking Penguin, 1999.

native american clan
Sun Bear, Wabun Wind, and Crysalis Mulligan. *Dancing with the Wheel.* New York: Simon & Schuster, 1991.

numerology
Crawford, Saffi, and G. Sullivan. *The Power of Birthdays.* New York: Ballantine, 1998.

palm reading
Webster, Richard. *Palm Reading for Beginners.* St. Paul, Minn.: Llewellyn Publications, 2000.

psychological profile
Kiersey, David W., and Marilyn Bates. *Please Understand Me.* Amherst, N.Y.: Prometheus, 1985.

seven types of intelligence
Gardner, Howard E. *Frames of Mind.* New York: Basic Books, 1993.

sun signs, quality and element
Crawford, Saffi, and G. Sullivan. *The Power of Birthdays.* New York: Ballantine, 1998.

notes